BLACK LANDSCAPES MATTER

BLACK LANDSCAPES MATTER

EDITED BY
Walter Hood
AND
Grace Mitchell Tada

University of Virginia Press
CHARLOTTESVILLE AND LONDON

University of Virginia Press
© 2020 by the Rector and Visitors of the University of Virginia
All rights reserved
Printed in the United States of America on acid-free paper

First published 2020

9 8 7 6 5 4 3 2

Library of Congress Cataloging-in-Publication Data

Names: Hood, Walter, editor. | Tada, Grace Mitchell, editor.
Title: Black landscapes matter / edited by Walter Hood and Grace Mitchell Tada.
Description: Charlottesville : University of Virginia Press, [2020] | Includes bibliographical references and
    index.
Identifiers: LCCN 2020020084 (print) | LCCN 2020020085 (ebook) | ISBN 9780813944852 (hardcover) |
    ISBN 9780813944869 (paperback) | ISBN 9780813944876 (epub)
Subjects: LCSH: African Americans—Social conditions. | Cultural landscapes—United States. |
    Landscapes—Symbolic aspects—United States. | Collective memory and city planning—United
    States. | United States—Race relations.
Classification: LCC E185.86 .B52559 2020 (print) | LCC E185.86 (ebook) | DDC 305.896/073—dc23
LC record available at https://lccn.loc.gov/2020020084
LC ebook record available at https://lccn.loc.gov/2020020085

Furthermore:
a program of the J. M. Kaplan Fund

Publication of this volume was assisted by a grant from Furthermore: a program of the J. M. Kaplan Fund.

Cover art: Redemption Mile, *Rosa Parks,* Detroit, Michigan, 2018. (Courtesy of Hood Design Studio)

CONTENTS

BLACK LANDSCAPES MATTER

INTRODUCTION

Walter Hood

Traditional Africans did not look forward to radical change or to a messianic age, but rather they "remembered" the homes of their forefathers, reestablished after death by their spirits and awaiting the souls of the living. . . . In this traditional African sacred cosmos, time was viewed as having scale of value. There were good times and bad times, times that were favorable for an activity and times that were inauspicious for that special action. These particular events that were tied to time were also tied further to place. Events should and have occurred at particular places on the earth, places that were auspicious for and tied to the event.
—Mechel Sobel, *The World They Made Together*

Black landscapes matter because they are prophetic. They tell the truth of the struggles and the victories of African Americans in North America. The landscape bears the detritus of diverse origins: from the plantation landscape of slavery, to freedman villages and new towns, to agrarian indentured servitude. To northern and western migrations for freedom, to segregated urban landscapes, and to an integrated pluralist society. Black landscapes illuminate the diaspora of free Africans from the Southern Hemisphere to North America. These landscapes are the prophecy of America; they tell us our future. Their constant erasure is a call to arms against concealment of the truth that some people don't want to know or see. Erasure is a call to arms to remember. Erasure allows people to forget, particularly those whose lives and actions are complicit.

The question "Do Black landscapes matter?" is intertwined in the colonial story of the Americas and their shadowed past. It is shared by all Americans, deeply ingrained in America's subconscious, and its landscapes. In the United States, the landscapes of my ancestors exist all around: from ocean to ocean, border to border, the diaspora of African Americans on the North American continent reaches far.

Imagine if the United States had built a monument to the end of the Civil War—to the end of slavery. Instead, as soon as the Civil War ended, the battlefield was declared a monument to the tens of thousands of soldiers who died. Not the war itself, or its causes, or its "heroes." At the dawning of freedom for African Americans, their emancipation was not imagined or viewed as something worthy of memorializing.

In the heterogeneous society of the United States, it takes time to work through memories. J. B. Jackson presents a framework that could help understand memory here. In *The Necessity for Ruins,* he writes:

> But there has to be that interval of neglect, there has to be discontinuity; it is religiously and artistically essential. That is what I mean when I refer to the necessity for ruins: ruins provide the incentive for restoration, and for a return to origins. There has to be (in our new concept of history) an interim of death or rejection before there can be renewal and reform. The old order has to die before there can be a born-again landscape. Many of us know the joy and excitement not so much of creating the new as of redeeming what has been neglected, and this excitement is particularly strong when the original condition is seen as holy and beautiful. . . . That is how we produce the cosmic scheme and correct history.[1]

Jackson is describing the landscape of preservation and commemoration, which can also provide ways for cultures to deal with cultural change and adaptation.

In previous times, Jackson writes, commemoration "determine[d] our actions in the years to come. . . . For centuries that is what monuments and feast days had been for: to remind us of obligations, religious or political, and keep us on the beaten path, loyal to tradition."[2]

Gettysburg, Jackson argues, is where the monument and the commemorative landscape changed. In the several decades following the war's end, monuments dedicated to the unknown soldiers from the North and South proliferated, and even to the Confederacy itself. These new monuments celebrate a different past, "not the past which history books describe, but a vernacular past, a golden age where there are no dates or names, simply a sense of the way it used to be, history as the chronicle of everyday experience."[3] It is this comment that offers a distinct lens through which we observe Black landscapes.

Here a second question emerges: are the places that I inhabit valued? Much of my life I have seen them mostly devalued. All around me, it is not these landscapes that are remembered, but the vernacular ones that Jackson mentions. In 2017, a southern politician, elucidating this view, remarked that the Black family under slavery was better off than they are presently, claiming that, in the past, Black people were "united" and "strong."[4] This vernacular past is celebrated in many manners, and, in many cases, the Black landscape is not a part of it. Middleton Place in Charleston, South Carolina, remembers its colonial gardens before it remembers its enslaved population and their contributions. The current conflicts surrounding the removal of the Civil War statues—those to which Jackson refers—celebrate the vernacular past. And the insistence on a vernacular past at the Lorraine Hotel in Memphis is manifest in the preference to talk about the African slavery diaspora rather than the murder of Dr. Martin Luther King Jr.

The past persists today as difficult burdens: the memory and guilt of institutionalized slavery, and the emancipation heritage. Memories document our historical presence in landscapes as subservient human beings, as segregated communities in a separate but equal cultural setting, and as integrated into the melting pot culture. Within this triad it is possible to see resilience, faith, optimism, and invention in the places and landscapes that African Americans made and occupy, but mostly these actions and places go forgotten. Are these memories too much for the country to bear? Are they too dark and heavy to bring forward for reconciliation?

Over the past 155 years, there have been moments when the country remembered. To name a few: the creation of the Freedmen's Bureau at the beginning of Reconstruction, the promise of forty acres and a mule, *Brown v. Board of Education,* the Civil Rights Act of 1964, and the Voting Rights Act of 1965. But there has always been a lag, a period of forgetting. Reconstruction's end, in 1877, by President Rutherford Hayes, immediately created a Jim Crow landscape in the South that persisted until the civil rights movement. Maybe a way to understand this pendulum of remembrance and neglect is through a 155-year timeline that begins with emancipation in 1865. Nearly forty years later, the National Association for the Advancement of Colored People was founded, and, in 1919, at the end of World War I, we were remembered for our service in the war. In the late 1980s and early 1990s, multiculturalism and hip-hop made us remember how "cool" Black is—until the neglect that followed. The election of Barack Obama, in 2008, demonstrated another period of remembrance followed by neglect, which led to the Black Lives Matter movement. But during these pauses or lapses we become apathetic, drunk from recent victories. Consequently, we are now in the midst of another period of neglect. The actions of some, who desire to erase the past, from immigration to civil rights, are forcing us to remember.

Black landscapes matter because they can be "born again." They exist all around us and are continuously resuscitated. Doing so requires care in how we exhume and resuscitate these landscapes to ensure that their resonance and power are not lost. Maybe some Black landscapes have become vernacular: we now have a Malcolm X Plaza, a Frederick Douglass Circle, an *Invisible Man* sculpture in Harlem, an MLK memorial in Washington, DC, and a plethora of new landscapes conserved to correct history. But we need something more powerful—not simply pedagogical, not a vernacular past, and not merely a chronicle. To correct history, we must see the original condition as "holy and beautiful." We must be audacious in what we bring forward.

Black landscapes matter because they are renewable. We can uncover, exhume, validate, and celebrate these landscapes through new narratives and stories that choose to return us to origins. The contested and the forgotten landscapes, renewed through a myriad of expressions, can give us incentives to obligations for years to come.

The period of neglect can be seen as a powerful "pregnant pause." It can be a time to develop new concepts of history without being thwarted by the old, which must die and be rejected. Culturally, this relates to the people and objects that preserve these memories. The interval of time is where memories are stored through reflexive borrowing, mimetic appropriations, exchanges, and inventions within the cultural landscape. Thus, when these memories are "born again," they can be prophetic. The nascent and latent landscapes that necessarily emerge from the neglected bear these memories and are mnemonic devices that can be triggered when we want to remember. Black voices are emerging today because we are in a period of neglect. How do we articulate and promote the acceptance and reconciliation of the cultural atrocities that accompany the American experiment? It is up to us to help America remember through our collective speech, writings, art, music, architecture, and landscapes.

Here is a call for new expressions that force reconciliation. I would argue that the times when opposition is loud—the periods of neglect—are the times when we renew. In these times, we must find ways to be outspoken, more audacious, and prophetic. Instead of being reactive, we should be proactive, preserving, conserving, and making more landscapes that are for us—Black landscapes that are resilient and forward-looking. Black landscapes that tell alternative stories and forge a new language for landscapes. Black landscapes that build on our local knowledge, a knowledge that attests to creativity and passion for inclusion.

The diverse voices assembled here represent "notes from the field." They are "memory workers," as the late Doria Dee Johnson expounded during a lecture a few years ago at UC Berkeley. These notes cover a wide geography, from the Carolinas to the Mississippi. They illuminate and convey that there are narratives and stories necessary to the current discourse. They help us to remember.

There is no single solution to the questions raised here, only a multiplicity of responses. How can art and design serve as mnemonic devices? How can environmental advocacy force us to remember the atrocities suffered living in unstable landscapes? Can new Black leadership in the planning and design of our cities create new narratives? And can pedagogy extend from the academic context into the world to constantly remind us of the collective voices that truly comprise America's cultural landscape?

The volume opens with personal accounts. Designer and educator Richard L.

Hindle offers a sobering view through a call to action based on the presidential election. Two essays share experiences that reflect racialized landscapes and their dynamics in the United States: that by designer and landscape historian Louise A. Mozingo, the other by urban planner Dr. Anna Livia Brand. As non-Black observers, they offer a set of narratives alternative to most of those that follow. Mozingo writes about her youthful experience of arrival to the United States via Rome, Italy, and describes her initial confrontation with race. She shares with us her personal observations of living in Washington, DC, and, in the nation's capital, the encounter with Blackness in the landscape. Brand documents the everyday and mundane life pre–Hurricane Katrina on the 4800 block of Camp Street, in New Orleans, over a fifteen-year period. Her acute observations illuminate the shifting and fragile displacement of people in a postcatastrophic context in which gentrification was cloaked in the politics of rebuilding.

North Carolina–based designer, educator, and environmental-justice advocate Kofi Boone takes us down a path of dissonance. Through the lens of the Black Lives Matter movement, Boone asks if we can we rethink landscape architecture. His compelling argument asserts the Black person as artisan, present in landscapes that range from plantations to historically Black college and university campuses, to political and economic urban spaces, to failed planned communities. He suggests that maybe art is at the center of the Black creative ethos, explained by three concepts: to be seen, to live with dignity, and to be connected. In reflecting on my own childhood in North Carolina, I consider how the diachronic nature of history has affected Black landscapes, and our memories of them, in the city of Charlotte.

From Detroit, Maurice Cox relates his personal journey as an architect, academic, politician, and activist through professional experiences in Virginia, New Orleans, and, finally, Detroit. *Who preserves Black landscapes?* he asks, presenting the Bayview community in rural Virginia as a place that offers ideas of self-determination, and New Orleans as a landscape shaped by a multicultural heritage. Cox's journey makes him seem destined for positions as planning director for the City of Detroit, Michigan, and commissioner of planning and development for the City of Chicago. For some, Detroit is the crucial testing ground for urbanism in the twenty-first century. How do we plan within a landscape of disinvestment and disenfranchisement of Black people, and, most of all, how do we not forget about Black people as a counterwave to new, predominantly white gentry returning to a place that they chose to leave behind?

Landscape architect, educator, and filmmaker Austin Allen reminds us of the struggle to define and maintain space that arises when we put our names on these spaces. Racial gaming has allowed our continued occupation of some places, he writes. Place can be elusive and improvisational, giving rise to rituals, rules, interpretations, and negotiations. As he travels through the southern landscape, long familiar to him, he offers examples that fully recognize histories and fictions. The "open city" concept, he suggests, can facilitate the preservation of place but, more importantly, can enable a transgressive set of negotiations. A photo-essay by photographer Lewis Watts—whose work has been influential in my own—portrays visually some of these same ideas.

Finally, as a case study, artist and civic-engagement facilitator Sara Daleiden discusses collaboration and agency as a tool for ethical cultural development within the context of a rail-to-trail project in Milwaukee, Wisconsin. The Harambee and Riverwest neighborhoods are spotlighted as she shifts land from the private realm to the public. The trail becomes the "thing" in the landscape that is a lens to figuratively navigate the neighborhood's marginalized predicaments and desires.

These "notes from the field" are a diverse collection of thoughts, provocations, and case studies. The landscapes that are everyday and mundane, commemorative, and community lifeways together argue for "culture" to be central to design, recognizing that places and environments are maintained, sustained, or transformed by the people and bureaucracies that control them. The essays are accompanied by images from my own design practice, demonstrating places where culture has been harnessed as a guiding design tenet. As the global context of place and culture becomes less distinct as heterogeneity blurs boundaries, it is crucial that we validate and nurture the existence of Black landscapes and spaces. Specific to the postcolonial landscapes that we inhabit, Black landscapes are forged within contested space, improvised and reshaped to allow Black people to thrive within a context of marginality and exclusion. But as our history assures us, Black people have built and shaped the American landscape in ways that we will never know. It is up to those of us in the field to continue to articulate and, most of all, develop a "prophetic aesthetic" to counter the colonial malaise so that we can remember and develop new futures from the power of the past.

Notes

1. J. B. Jackson, *The Necessity for Ruins* (Amherst: University of Massachusetts Press, 1980), 102.

2. Jackson, *The Necessity for Ruins,* 93.

3. Jackson, *The Necessity for Ruins,* 94–95.

4. German Lopez, "Roy Moore: America 'Was Great at the Time When Families Were United—Even Though We Had Slavery,'" Vox, December 8, 2017, www.vox.com/policy-and-politics/2017/12/7/16748038/roy-moore-slavery-america-great.

PART I

Calls to Action

AS AMERICAN AS BASEBALL (AND CENTRAL PARK)

Richard L. Hindle

During the preelection milieu of 2016, discussions of Black landscapes provoked timely contemplation about race in the built environment, and an exploration of the significant role Black lives, thoughts, and actions have had in the shaping of the American landscape. After November 2016, when the American people elected "The First White President," the discussion developed an unwelcomed, though palpable, poignancy.[1] Illusions of a postracial America inspired by the presidency of Barack Hussein Obama had only partially masked the deep-rooted divisions that have separated, defined, and haunted the melting pot since colonial slavery. I counted myself among the optimistic, if naïve, masses who believed the iconography and message of America's first Black president could help mend centuries of institutional and embodied racism. I was wrong.

In the days, weeks, months, and years since Donald J. Trump's election, the not-not-racist past of the world's greatest democracy has rapidly caught up with the present in a surprisingly virulent postmodern form. White nationalists carried discount-store tiki torches to defend statues of Robert E. Lee in Charlottesville; live Facebook video captured the murder of a Black man by Minnesota police and replays online; criminal charges were brought against Michigan state employees for

The Lifeways plan illustrates how the cultural and ecological history of a place can inform existing and new landscape patterns. The historic lot lines running perpendicular to Horlbeck Creek were planted to become fifteen-foot easements to enable drainage, provide new tree patches, and allow free play for neighborhood kids. (Hood Design Studio, Phillips Lifeways Plan, Mount Pleasant, South Carolina, 2006)

poisoning the residents of Flint through divestment in public infrastructure; and banners reading "Racism Is as American as Baseball" reached millions in the form of internet memes. It is not a coincidence that most, if not all, of this drama is unfolding in physical, and virtual, public realms. These are the spaces and places where *one* encounters *another* and must acknowledge a shared history and proximity. Herein lies the key to *why Black landscapes matter* to all of us.

The notion of a *Black landscape* cuts deep to the core of American history, pres-

RICHARD L. HINDLE

ent and future. African slave labor built many of the earliest colonial landscapes, from the plantations of the Southeast to the first levees that protected New Orleans against the Mississippi River's fluctuating waters. Even beloved spaces, such as Central Park in New York City, may be understood through the lens of *Black landscapes*, having displaced the African American community of Seneca Village prior to construction of the park in the mid-nineteenth century.[2] As a white man born in England and raised in New York, I have only ever known America as a heterogeneous mix of races, cultures, and ideas—a radical departure from the rural town on the Blackwater Estuary where I spent the first years of my life. Yet for all the diversity of this country, it is striking how polarized and divided it remains, and how little we know about the *Black landscapes* that are inseparable from the American landscape we all share. Maybe it's time we all take a knee and look around.

Notes

1. Ta-Nehisi Coates, "The First White President," *Atlantic,* October 2017.
2. Douglas Martin, "A Village Dies, a Park Is Born," *New York Times,* January 31, 1997.

INSISTING ON ANSWERS

Louise A. Mozingo

In the summer of 1968, when I turned ten, my family moved to Arlington, Virginia, across the Potomac River from Washington, DC. We had spent the previous few months at an idyllic, if isolated, small military base in the Catoctin Mountains of Maryland, close to Camp David. Before that we had lived for more than four years in Rome, Italy. While living in Rome, we spent summers and Christmas with my maternal grandparents in Gorizia, a town of fifty thousand and an elegant gem in the Veneto region of northeastern Italy.

Having arrived in Italy before my fifth birthday, a sense of continuity about my own life came into being while there. I began to understand myself as living in a city and a town with streets, buildings, sidewalks, shops, restaurants, markets, cafés, piazzas, and churches (many churches), part of a family, but also of a society, inhabiting a particular place and using it in a particular way. I was neither a tourist nor a traveler, but the child of an Italian mother and an American father who first arrived in Rome in July 1944. I became fluent not only in the language of where I was growing up but also in the customs and manners of moving through urban space, most deliciously on foot. I would pause to buy prosciutto, get a gelato, nod to a neighbor, gaze at a fountain, admire a facade, ogle shoes in a store window, wonder at the

Christmas fair, and, on special occasions, enjoy a treat at an outdoor café, winter or summer.

In the Italy of my childhood, the public realm provided endless entertainment, a place to observe the built and the human mingling in alluring ways. A place to feel pretty in my new dress, witness the pageantry of my religion, tag along with adults in grown-up activities, and, most happily, to see everybody out—talking, walking, shopping, looking, sitting, and sipping, participating indiscriminately in the spectacle of everyday life. While Italians intensely protected their private realm, reserving the home only for the intimates of one's clan, the public realm formed an equitable, free domain where the fraught and inevitable tensions of family life could be left behind.

The move to a suburban house in Arlington displaced my daily life in many ways, but most palpably in the way I inhabited the place I lived. From the neighborhood's endless, shut-tight dwellings, carefully separated by trees and lawn, no one emerged, except the occasional zooming automobile. In the postwar subdivision manner, no sidewalks lined the roadways, and, in any case, there was nothing within walking distance of interest, except more houses. Shopping involved long rides stuck in the car, large parking lots, and vast fluorescently lit indoor spaces. After the pomp of Rome, our suburban church in its own lake of parking seemed dispiriting, at best.

I cannot remember if I voiced my disconcertion, but one Sunday afternoon my father drove us into Washington, to Bassin's, which, years earlier, in 1961, had opened as Washington's first sidewalk café. We were the only customers. I began to understand that different rules governed the American public realm. This was the fall of 1968, and Bassin's stood short blocks away from the site of the King assassination uprising earlier in the year. Whether the National Guard troops remained by that point did not matter, as no one, Black or white, strolled along the sidewalks, the curfew and the fear long since internalized.

The idea that there were places that some could go, and others could not, made no sense to me, yet adults, the media, and the kids at school talked about "sections" of DC and Arlington. Our neighbors would complacently state with a knowing look that that they would never venture "downtown." As I spent the 1970s visiting relatives in my father's homeplace of Selma, North Carolina, the textile town of four thousand that he escaped, the racist divides of the American landscape became excruciatingly obvious. The railroad split the small settlement, sequestering the Black residents on the "other side of the tracks," and violation of these confines aroused obvious suspicion among white residents. I have never forgotten the exclamation of the local district court judge as a Black man walked down the Selma street where the judge and my aunts lived: "What's that burrhead doing on this side of town?" Given that I was within earshot, I knew the judge chose a racist slur that was, in his mind, restrained. Still, I recognized the threat: a Black man walking on that street was doing so at his own peril.

Back in Arlington, my parents, much to their credit, continued to present Washington, DC, as a desirable place. My mother and I took the slow bus to F Street to visit the grand old department stores, specialty shops, and Reeve's Bakery, rather than to the new suburban Tyson's Corner Mall and its food court. An early life in Italy and the defiant optimism of those downtown DC forays instilled in me an enduring faith in the possibilities of the public realm as a place of common ground. My eventual commitment to landscape architecture emerged as my delight in urbanity coupled with the love of all things botanical, color in fall leaves and spring bloom a singular redeeming feature of all those Arlington suburban yards.

As Washington, DC, knit back together in the aftermath of the King assassination, ever so slowly, the reality of an urbane, inclusive public realm of explicit goodwill seemed possible. On a blessed summer evening in 2011, I visited DC's Columbia Heights, one of the centers of the 1968 uprising. In the wide sidewalks and plazas around the Metro station at Fourteenth and Irving Streets, everyone was out— Black, brown, and white attracted by a newly opened "urban" Target (no parking lot), useful service shops, every mode of food spilling onto sidewalks, a walk-in fountain where kids screeched with delight in sprays of water, and lots of places to sit and hang out. When I saw a line of elderly folks in wheelchairs wheeled out to the curb from an adjacent long-term care facility to take in the glee of the passing scene, I thought the perniciousness of cities divided could, indeed, be overcome: Rome '66 meets "I Have a Dream" '63.

I was not entirely wrong, perhaps, but I certainly was not entirely right. As recent events make amply clear, the Selma judge's narrow-eyed verdict of decades ago still prevails in too many instances, too often, and tragically justifies the most egregious violence possible, the killing of human life. We remain wretchedly divided in place and therefore at heart.

The essays that follow ask exigent questions of us who value, design, and tend the collective metropolitan spaces we, theoretically, share. We must insist on answers; there is urgent work to do.

BLACK LANDSCAPES MATTER ... THEN AND NOW, HERE AND EVERYWHERE

Anna Livia Brand

For Maxine Adams

The 4800 block of Camp Street in New Orleans is nestled just above the hustle of Magazine Street. It is a block of one- and two-story homes, most of which were built in the late 1800s. Some are renovated, some not. Some have a fresh coat of paint, some not. Some have flipped to new, white property owners due to the forces of post-Katrina gentrification, but many have not. Those that have not are still held by Black homeowners who have owned the homes for two to three generations. Many families live together, a blend of generations in one home. Grandparents watch out for grandkids playing on the sidewalk. Grandchildren now grown bring their children to play, their chorus echoing down the street on the same sidewalk where their fathers or mothers once played. Neighbors watch out for one another: they know each other across generations and across the street. Neighbors watched out for Tyrone's grandmother, Ms. Petey, who, in her later years, tended to wander. Neighbors watch out for Ms. Adams, whose family built a ramp to the front porch to accommodate her wheelchair, allowing her to come down to the sidewalk and cruise the block. In the hot summer sun, Maxine Adams stops her wheelchair in the shade of the tree at the end of the block outside my house, talking with and sharing the shade with those of us who choose to pause alongside her.

I became neighbors with the folks on Camp Street and lived with them for nearly fifteen years. It was Tyrone, Ms. Petey, Ms. Adams, Mrs. Cummings, Dwayne, Edward, and others on this street who created and shaped, over generations, the everyday Black landscape of this block. Here, the entanglements of racialized prosperity and hardship are best understood in the sharing of everyday battles and the collective practice of making-do and surviving in the space between our front doors. Nearly every home had a front porch, where a chair—or two or three—positioned neighbors to talk with one another, to be with one another in the liminal, sacred space between private homes and the street. From your porch and down the street, you saw which kids were outside to play on a hot, humid summer day. From your porch and across the street, you saw Tyrone waiting for a customer at his improvised driveway car wash, talking with a neighbor who no longer lived on but still visited the block. From your porch and down the street, you saw Ms. Adams on her porch warming herself in the sun on one of the blindingly beautiful southern days. You knew then that you could walk down and say hello, see how she was feeling that day. You knew then that it had been too many days since you had heard her voice. From Mrs. Cummings's porch, you were given a soft, pale-blue set of booties and hat that she knit for your first child. Here, on her porch, she shared with you her radiant smile when she learned your second son's name, Arthur—her husband's name. From your own porch, two doors down, you saw Dwayne catching a smoke on his porch, and you hollered down to see when his son, Jeron, would be home to play with your kids, Luka and Artie. You heard Jeron's full-of-life voice carry into your front room, and the kids would pile out the door, pulling on shoes or not, getting outside as quickly as they could. Jeron, Luka, Artie, Grey (Elly's daughter), Baylon (Maxine's great-grandson and Edward's son), and Olivia (from down the block) formed a loose gang of mostly Black children from ages two to twelve who made cardboard swords, rode bikes and scooters, and ran the block until collapsing, exhausted, on one of our porches to cool down.

The block was—is—full of life. It bursts with a subtle rhythm that speaks to why Black landscapes matter *then,* when Ms. Adams and her husband bought the house, and *now,* as they are reexposed to new rounds of displacement and land vulnerability. When the Adamses bought their house, they were setting in motion and in place a new landscape. Originally a part of the Avart Plantation, the land upon which the Adamses' house stood was a plantation cultivated by slave labor. After 1829, Louis Bouligny developed the land into a neighborhood that was annexed by the city in 1870. When the Adamses came to the area in the 1960s, they, along with other Black homeowners on this block of sixteen homes, helped establish a Black landscape no longer solely defined by slavery and racial segregation. They held the space and the land and, for more than forty years, they held a Black landscape intact through everyday acts and a spatial praxis of mutuality and love. The spaces of the sidewalk, porch, front stoop, and front door are sacred elements of this Black landscape, and they matter more than their sometimes-eroding materiality can reveal. The being-together-in-one-place-ness of Black landscapes matters. It mattered then when the Adamses purchased their home, and it matters now. It mattered then because it transformed the trajectory of this place from a space where slaves were held and brutalized to one where Black people owned and held the land. It mattered then for establishing the generations-long ownership and understanding of place, for locating a safe home amid still-ongoing, though changing, racisms. It mattered then for signifying hope in a city born of plantation geographies and land theft.

Black landscapes matter now, though we also know that the patterns set in motion in a post–civil rights city are slowly, and sometimes quickly, being eroded or shifted. In New Orleans, some of these shifts were evident before Katrina hit in 2005. For instance, the outer limits of Tremé, the oldest African American neighborhood, were slowly being eroded by bed-and-breakfasts catering to French Quarter tourism and the city's tourist economy. The larger Uptown neighborhood, where this Camp Street block sits, had also been experiencing the slow shifts of gentrification, though largely not this block until after Katrina. In 1970, the Black population in the census tract of this block on Camp Street peaked, reaching over 55 percent of the total tract population. By 1990, it had dipped to nearly 46 percent and, by 2000, to 36 percent. My own presence as a white renter signified some of these shifts in the early 2000s and signaled what would become increasingly evident after the storm. Hurricane Katrina increased the pace of Black displacement that was slowly happening across the city. Since 2005, Black landscapes that had been held intact—some since the 1890s, others since the 1960s—have been worn away,

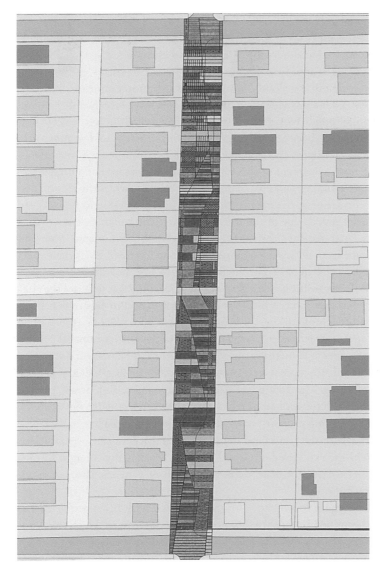

As part of William McDonough's Cradle
to Cradle project in the Lower Ninth
Ward, a series of excavations explored
performance-based street landscapes.
(Hood Design Studio, Pilot Project of
Tennessee Street, Lower Ninth Ward,
New Orleans, Louisiana, 2009)

eroding Black spatial logics of liberation and claims to land held and loved. It is as if the pace of whiteness picks up in these moments of extreme trauma and inundates Black landscapes with newly revised spatial logics of clearance, dispossession, and displacement that forget, appropriate, absent, and silence Blackness.

4800 Camp Street did not flood during Katrina. Although some of the homes were impacted by the hurricane-force winds, residents were largely able to come back to their homes long before those in areas of the city that bore the most devastating floodwaters. Yet, between 2000 and 2010, this census tract lost more than three hundred Black residents and gained more than two hundred white residents. White residents, now 74 percent of this tract's population, represent a higher percentage of the tract's total population than they did in 1940, when the city first recorded census information at the tract level. And while Black residents now occupy a significantly lower percentage of the tract's total population (19.8 percent) than they did in 1940 (39.6 percent), the statistics most notably demonstrate how long this Black landscape has held space here and the shifting nature of Black landscapes in a post–civil rights, now neoliberalizing, landscape. While the numbers represent important, if not slowly shifting, demographics of place, they also indicate the challenges we collectively face to keep Black landscapes intact and to ensure that Black geographies are all geographies.

Black landscapes mattered then, in the mid-twentieth-century hopeful context of redefining landscapes as something other than a southern plantation born of racial capitalism. Black landscapes matter now, though the topographies and geographies of race are shifting. Ms. Adams had to sell her house on Camp Street, the one she and her husband, Edward, had purchased and made a home in. Between her medical bills and the rising property taxes, she could not afford to live in the home and on the block where she had raised her children and where her grandchildren and great-grandchildren still lived or visited. She and her daughter bought a house in Gentilly, one of the last affordable places to live in New Orleans. She, too, is one of the people now gone.

In the days leading up to her move, she was afflicted with heart problems and anxiety about the impending move. "No one knows me there. Here, everyone knows me and looks out for me," she told me. "Here, I don't have to worry."

Ms. Adams is one of many Black residents in the shifting Black geographies across the United States. Her worry speaks to the precariousness of Black geographic claims. Yet she and Camp Street also represent an alternative to the temporal and geographic repatterning of dislocation that erodes Black presence in the landscape. The foundation of her worry—the *they* who know her on *this block,* with its rhythms of front porches and calls across the street—speaks to the ways that Black landscapes collide space and time to create something other than being raced, other than being delineated and predefined by the color of one's skin. Black landscapes are created out of apartheid racial systems—slave ship, auction block, plantation, Jim Crow, redlining, block busting, discrimination, clearance, abandonment, violence—but they are not solely of these systems. They are racialized, but they are not solely contoured by race and racism. Outside of these systems, they resound with other possible futures.

These futures point toward the possibilities of tuning in and turning up the rhythm and spaciousness of everyday Black landscapes so the forces of racism and its interlocking and mutating spatial logics do not limit what and how we see, nor how we understand and amplify this rhythm and spaciousness. The everyday moments of Black landscapes speak to these futures by letting light in, voice in, some other rhythm in. The beauty of the sky over the Mississippi levee in New Orleans's Lower Ninth Ward is a Black landscape that pauses time. Here, we step outside of the denigration of a lower-income (yes) but still beautiful, inhabited Black landscape. Here, folks also holler to one another across porches. Here, folks know one another and one another's families by the house and property that they live in. Each home is a story of creating space and community. Each home, worn porch, and sloping concrete stoop etch and evidence lives lived, and life persisting.

Black landscapes bring the past into the present. In New Orleans's Tremé neighborhood, painted murals now grace the underpass columns of the I-10 expressway, whose construction in the late 1960s destroyed the Black business core on North Claiborne Avenue. Here, a mural of La Branche Pharmacy, an everyday place in early twentieth-century Tremé that Emile La Branche, a Black pharmacist, opened in 1907, reminds us what was created and set in motion when he trained other Black pharmacists. Here, murals of Black residents calling to one another across stoops in Tremé, and the presence of the Urban League, the NAACP, the Standard Life Insurance Company, the Mardi Gras Indians, and Ernie K-Doe's Mother-In-Law Lounge, speak to the endurance and spaciousness of Black landscapes across different temporalities. Here, now, second-line parades and Mardi Gras Indians claim these spaces through sound, movement, and inhabitation. Here, now, the past connects to the present and therefore to the future: it hollers across time that Black landscapes cannot be fully eroded, it echoes in and across the porch, the street, the underpass, the sidewalk, the stoop—and its resonance is luminous. North Claiborne Avenue collapses time to tell us the importance of not forgetting history in our search for some other future, and reminds us that Black landscapes are maps toward a different world—they are maps toward a geography of liberation. Camp Street disassembles the plantation and creates a different world.

Black landscapes are then and now, here and everywhere—from the house and the tempo of porches and stoops to the larger landscapes of business and cultural corridors and spaces where Blackness is active, living, creative, remembering, inventing. The down-the-street landscape of 4800 Camp Street matters for its patterns, fundamental in the lives of its residents. It extended to include the Black music at Benny's Blues Bar a few blocks away, where the Nevilles, who lived nearby on Valence, off Camp Street, played. It extended to the corner store on Magazine and to the market on Prytania, and to the bar around the corner. North Claiborne Avenue matters for its history of Black-owned everyday spaces—businesses and social clubs that styled day and night into something undefined by segregation. North Claiborne expands backward and forward in time, connecting memory to the living present, making claims on the future. Black landscapes along Thirty-Fifth and Forty-Seventh Streets in Chicago's South Side matter for the ways that Black-owned businesses and cultural institutions should have challenged our notions of blight and the ensuing erosive unsettling of these landscapes. Black landscapes matter in Houston's Third Ward, where artists and residents center Black lives and revalue the Black vernacular landscape of shotgun homes into a new space of Black spatial praxis.

Black landscapes activate present-day life. They are palpable in the fight to keep intact the Claiborne corridor for New Orleans's Black community. They are evident in the continuous practice of inhabiting streets and sidewalks in New Orleans's living second-line parade tradition. They are manifested in the construction of a platform for residents to see the beauty of the Lower Nine's Bayou Bienvenue. They are apparent in the Lower Nine's House of Dance and Feathers and Tremé's Backstreet Cultural Museum that hold space for Mardi Gras Indians, Social Aid & Pleasure Clubs, and Skull and Bone Gangs, all of which give room to the creative, hard, triumphant work toward freedom.[1]

Black landscapes—then and now, here and everywhere—teach us about a different rhythm of calling across the street, washing cars in the driveway, sitting on porches and talking, and kids running up and down a block. They teach us about being human and connecting over a plate of greens, corn bread, and black-eyed peas to ring in the new year in New Orleans. They resound, from Mrs. Cummings's handmade creations, to Jeron's exuberant and thoughtful energy, to Tyrone's keeping of the block, to Ms. Adams's love for her block. Their pasts and presents, their then-ness and their now-ness, their here-ness and everywhere-ness, accumulate and carry forward the memory and possibility of other possible futures.

Notes

1. House of Dance and Feathers, accessed October 30, 2018, http://houseofdanceandfeathers .org; Backstreet Cultural Museum, "About Us: History," accessed October 30, 2018, www.back streetmuseum.org/about-us/4544606754.

PART II

Practicing Culture

THE EVERYDAY AND MUNDANE

Black people engage in everyday and mundane actions that go unnoticed most of the time. These habitual experiences condition us to our familiar: taking a trip to the corner store, hanging out on the stoop or porch, meeting friends at the park or corner, driving to work. Over time, these occurrences either open one's eyes to their context, or create narrow blinders that omit the unwanted. Through repetition and pattern, we edit what and how we want to experience our surroundings.

The environment hosts dormant sculptures, bound to their context by clear, definable functions. We experience these sculptures every day in our mundane acts of life. These "sculptures," or "things," are objects omnipresent in the built environment. They are often ignored, but, in most cases, they are all we have: power boxes, light posts, stop signs, curbs, gutters, and street signs. At the larger scale, the freeway or overpass are axiomatic structures. To see them clearly and become conscious of their material possibility, their normative functions must be disregarded. Attention to the everyday and mundane recognizes what already exists around us, and activates the space between its "things" and its people. Activating the mundane is an opportunity to see and experience the beauty and utility of the things in our life.

The I-580 freeway spans above Splash Pad Park as a simple, nonobjective composition of roadway infrastructure. Below, sidewalks, walls, curbs, and parking interrogate a park's makeup. (Hood Design Studio, Splash Pad Park, Oakland, California, 2003)

THE EVERYDAY AND MUNDANE

The Saturday market activates the mundane, everyday landscape of the I-580 freeway. (Hood Design Studio, Splash Pad Park, Oakland, California, 2003)

Residents advocated for five Black heroes (the "five M's") to span Seventh Street: Madam C. J. Walker, Malcolm X, Martin Luther King Jr., Maya Angelou, and Nelson Mandela. Barack Obama and the late Esther Mabry (of the West Oakland blues and jazz club Esther's Orbit Room) also grace the gateway. Like pictures that once populated Black family living rooms, the heroes are now seen every day. (Hood Design Studio, 7th Street Dancing Lights and Gateway, Oakland, California, 2012)

A close-up view of the Seventh Street Gateway features an image of Barack Obama. (Hood Design Studio, 7th Street Dancing Lights and Gateway, Oakland, California, 2012)

The Bayview Opera House embraced its past and encouraged its future when it opened its landscape to the neighborhood. Now, floating ramps enable ADA access and allow programming to extend outside, facilitating daily use by the community. (Hood Design Studio, Bayview Opera House, San Francisco, California, 2016)

Young Black children welcome the historic Bayview Opera House's newly accessible walkway. (Hood Design Studio, Bayview Opera House, San Francisco, California, 2016)

A large map adorned a wall in the Memminger district, illustrating the Ashley and Cooper River landscapes where rice production by enslaved Africans transformed the waterways. Rice grown on pallets within hundreds of tubs created a wetland in a paved elementary school play yard. Within weeks, an emergent wetland ecology invited birds and amphibian life. In Charleston's swamplands, the role of the enslaved African in the production of Carolina Gold Rice became immediately clear. (Walter Hood, Frances Whitehead, Ernesto Pujol, and Kendra Hamilton, Water Table, Charleston, South Carolina, 2004)

LIFEWAYS

Black communities maintain, conserve, and preserve places and spaces that reinforce their particular ways of living. Within the American diaspora, this "way of life" can be idiosyncratic, countercultural, or non-normative. It's a "way of life" that is truly American, suggesting individual freedom and choice. Reinforcing individualism and collective diversity, it suggests a willingness to validate an array of norms and actions.

We are constantly engaged in the processes of acculturation and assimilation. Rarely is difference validated, unless it is economically profitable. Urban design and planning projects often seek to organize, tidy, and homogenize environments through standards that can be easily understood by all. But if the focus is given to unique ways of life, alternative narratives can emerge that describe how people live in different places.

The Coal Seam Trail in Pittsburgh's Hill District brought back a lifeway in a neighborhood plagued by disinvestment and abandonment. The landscape was once a place of labor (coal extraction) and, later, a Black working- and middle-class neighborhood. The value of mid- to upper-class suburban communities is directly related to its landscape context. In the Hill District, it was possible for the successional urban landscape that emerged to have the same value and become a new lifeway. (Hood Design Studio, Greenprint, Pittsburgh, Pennsylvania, 2010)

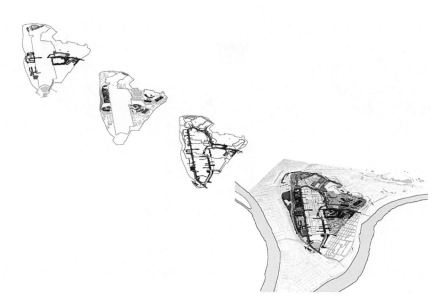

The Greenprint
established a
simple logic to the
Hill's successional
landscape: "the
woods and the
village." Like an
inverted Central
Park diagram, the
woods created a
donut to buffer the
community from the
Monongahela and
Allegheny Rivers.
(Hood Design
Studio, Greenprint,
Pittsburgh,
Pennsylvania, 2010)

Along a busy pedestrian walk, new stormwater capture systems echoed the formal extraction methods of coal. They remind us every day of the history: the labor that created communities, and the ongoing natural processes of these circumstances along Herron Ave. (Hood Design Studio, Greenprint, Pittsburgh, Pennsylvania, 2010)

Philadelphia's Asian Arts Initiative wanted to transform Pearl Street alley into a park. A three-hundred-bed shelter for (predominantly Black) men was located in the alley, and Hood Design Studio questioned the impulse for transformation. In response, the Studio made furniture and organized a community feast for everyone. (Hood Design Studio, Pearl Street Feast + Alley Galleries, Philadelphia, Pennsylvania, 2013)

Conversations at the Pearl Street Feast strove to inspire small infrastructural changes that would reinforce lifeways in the alleys. In contrast to the boarded windows along the Pearl Street alley, the *Fresh Windows* installation suggested that the simple act of opening windows could reimplement social and industrious uses on the backside of the block. The alley could become a central part of people's lives rather than a place to avoid. (Hood Design Studio, Pearl Street Feast + Alley Galleries, Philadelphia, Pennsylvania, 2013)

An extensive community engagement process revealed different lifeways of Black youth in East Palo Alto, California. Breaking stereotypical characterizations, their lifeways extended beyond the marginalized community and into a regional landscape where performance occurred every day. (Hood Design Studio, EPACENTER Arts, East Palo Alto, California, 2016)

A community painting project temporarily called attention to a simple lifeway in Opa Locka, Florida, where a barren roadway stretched for a mile without any landscape amenities beyond signage and infrastructure. Utilizing all social resources—the Coast Guard, school-age kids, and local adults—the street was painted to reinforce the town's Moorish aesthetic. The effort showed bureaucrats that transformations were possible, no matter how small. (Hood Design Studio, Site/Cite, Opa Locka, Florida, 2015)

The Rosa Parks neighborhood was centered along Twelfth Street, the site of the 1967 Rebellion. The new lifeway plan utilized the cultural history of the neighborhood, redesigning Twelfth Street as Redemption Mile that connected to existing cultural elements, such as the Algiers Motel and Gordon Parks memorial. Elements included: (*a*) an art house; (*b*) a community house; (*c*) a tree allée; (*d*) the Virginia Park Plaza containing a canopy-covered market and adjacent lawn; (*e*) sports fields; (*f*) the painted Rosa Parks Boulevard, open to pedestrians and bikes; (*g*) a sculpture garden; (*h*) the neighborhood gateway; (*i*) tree nurseries; (*j*) nursery house; and (*k*) greenhouses. (Hood Design Studio, Rosa Parks, Detroit, Michigan, 2018)

Vacant houses were excavated to reveal new opportunities for use, relocating certain programs and activities from the large community center into the community. (Hood Design Studio, Rosa Parks, Detroit, Michigan, 2018)

Redemption Mile would close half of the boulevard and return it to the community for commemoration and daily use. (Hood Design Studio, Rosa Parks, Detroit, Michigan, 2018)

COMMEMORATION

As time passes, things accumulate around us: buildings, vegetation, objects, and even space. This accumulation is typical in cities as their dynamic engages specific environmental, political, social, and cultural change. In many places, the accretion occurs unmitigated, literally revealing their stories: the moors in Cordoba, the detritus of the Roman Empire, and, in the Americas in particular, the physical echoes of colonialism.

In many cases in the United States, when time comes to change, Black landscapes are wiped clean, leaving little to commemorate what came before. Choosing to honor only events and actions that occur at the extremes of human experience mutes the common and mundane. The acknowledgment of a wall, a street, or a piece of infrastructure honors those who occupied a precise place in time. To commemorate those things is to remember them.

Within a diverse culture, a palimpsest—the layering of physical surfaces that reveals the passing of time—is crucial for the inclusion of Black groups within the public realm. Environments should be layered in their physical construction, becoming a collage of all the lives that have been lived in a place.

A set of fragmented concrete sculptural walls commemorate Nashville events that occurred during the civil rights movement. (Hood Design Studio, Witness Walls, Nashville, Tennessee, 2017)

More than 40 percent of the African diaspora in the United States today traces their enslaved ancestry to Gadsden's Wharf. Here, an infinity-edge fountain marks the arrival threshold between land and sea, ritualizing and reinterpreting the sacred ground of the wharf. (Hood Design Studio, visualization as of 2018, International African American Museum, Charleston, South Carolina)

The memorial to African ancestry collapses time, bringing us within reach of both the past and the future: it is a means by which to connect to West African ancestry, to the continuation of culture and tradition, and to future possibilities. (Hood Design Studio, visualization as of 2018, International African American Museum, Charleston, South Carolina)

PART III

Notes from the Field

ENABLING CONNECTIONS TO EMPOWER PLACE

The Carolinas

Kofi Boone

Our very presence is a disruption.
—bell hooks, *Yearning: Race, Gender, and Cultural Politics*

Introduction

Once again, a national conversation is under way about why and how race plays a role in the broader functions of American society. Although it has numerous antecedents, this current conversation is driven by two proximate flashpoints: the circumstances that led to the election of two-term President Barack Obama, and the aftermath climaxing in the election of President Donald Trump. The election of President Obama ushered in a short-lived glimmer of hope; perhaps the country was prepared to reconsider deeply set racial animus and move on to acknowledge the abilities and contributions of Black people to American society. But the resultant rise of local, state, and, eventually, national Republican control in the majority of nonurban U.S. places, prompted by explicitly stoking race-based fear in white communities through targeted messaging, serves as a reminder that there is work to do. This era of "whitelash" has taken many aback and forced the search for new counterstrategies.[1]

Although the Trump era heralded the erosion of numerous policies that protect human rights, some immediate and visceral threats, particularly to Black and brown people, became global news during the Obama years. Most notably, the police murder of Michael Brown in Ferguson, Missouri, in 2011, gave voice to coalitions that had been working across the country with the announcement of the Black Lives Matter movement.[2] Black Lives Matter (BLM) has become a profoundly influential American protest movement. Building from contemporary mobilization strategies developed through Occupy Wall Street, as well as from historical ones like those of Ella Baker and the Student Non-Violent Coordinating Committee (SNCC), BLM leveraged the police murder of Michael Brown into an international movement. BLM made a deceptively simple proposition: you cannot have a just society if an unarmed Black person's life is not protected from state-sanctioned murder.

The simplicity is deceptive because there are no spatial signifiers correlated to police killings of Black people. The research suggests that the disproportionate use of lethal force against Black people by the police is driven by the perceptions and prejudices of police and the categorical identification of Black people as threats to safety. Michael Brown was a working-class teenager murdered in Ferguson, a small, low-income suburb of St. Louis. Prince Jones, the concluding focal point of Ta-Nehisi Coates's contemporary masterpiece *Between the World and Me,* was an upper-middle-class college student murdered in Washington, DC.[3] This murder manifests bell hooks's observation in "Postmodern Blackness" that "Our very presence is a disruption."[4] The current use of language about "the Black body" as the indicator of health and safety, as well as the effectiveness of policies affecting Black people collectively, is an important leveler that makes politics personal.

Additionally, BLM's intersectional leadership reflects the contemporary re-definition of politics, whereby formally decentralized people are centered as examples of their own systems. hooks anticipated this trend by describing how reclaiming and appropriating the definitions of "margin" and "center" in the context of white supremacy are in themselves acts of resistance. In the case of BLM, the populations most vulnerable to violence, including police violence, are Black and brown LGBTQ people. BLM, however, has focused primarily on making visible the vulnerability of Black and brown individuals regardless of gender. Their view from their own "center" has demonstrated inclusivity while unapologetically placing those formerly marginalized as their most vocal exponents. In the 2016 post-election season, BLM focused on elevating and supporting a new generation of local candidates and leadership.

Despite BLM's innovations in the political and social landscape, some have questioned the long-term impact of BLM on national policy affecting Black people and all Americans. In an attempt to move from nonviolent direct action to more traditional political tools, BLM created a comprehensive platform now being championed by the Movement for Black Lives that extended to areas of health, safety, and well-being where Black people live. Some have been disappointed by their use of more mainstream and established directions, including the advocacy of affordable housing, jobs, and educational opportunities for vulnerable communities.

Their progression, however, moving from the scale of "the Black body" to the levers shaping the communities impacting Black bodies, offers exciting possibilities for Black planners and designers working with Black communities. In *The Aesthetics of Equity*, Craig L. Wilkins describes myriad issues impacting how deeply set inequities facing Black designers and communities might be addressed.[5] Among his many observations is one that ties back to hooks: "Many narratives of resistance struggle from slavery to the present share an obsession with the politics of space. . . . Indeed, Black folks equated freedom with passage into a life where they would have the right to exercise control over space on their own behalf, where they would imagine, design, and create spaces that would respond to the needs of their lives, their communities, their families."[6] But BLM, as with many similar efforts, does not tie these broader aspirations to an awareness of the potential of Black designers and planners. Wilkins lays out many of the reasons for the disconnect between Black and brown empowerment writ large, and the professions charged with giving form to the places that enable these processes.

Although there is no mention of the built environment professions as a component of community empowerment, there is a large amount of creative production around BLM and its issues. A video that went viral combines "The Mannequin Challenge" with BLM social commentary; it also illustrates a high level of design thinking applied to contemporary issues.[7] Music, fashion, film, and other forms of media all reflect the energy of the time. But where are the built environment professions? And where is landscape architecture?

Renowned scholar Mark Anthony Neal recently moderated a conversation at Duke University between cinematographer Arthur Jafa and celebrated cultural critic Greg Tate. The conversation recovered the need to reconnect to the makers of Black cultural artifacts. Jafa, the acclaimed cinematographer of Julie Dash's *Daughters of the Dust,* described the Black creative ethos as "somewhere between holding your tongue and speaking in tongues." He characterized the breadth of Black expression as grounded in the spectrum between the sacred and the profane, in the manner of Amiri Baraka's *Blues People,* making no distinction between "high" and "low" cultural practices.[8] Jafa observed that the innovative and avant-garde creative expressions present across Black popular media culture, music, and fashion indicate that the spirit driving the making of powerful artifacts is as strong as ever. He made a point, however, of excluding architecture (and by extension landscape architecture) from this phenomenon.

In Jafa's mind, the built environment professions do not operate in the same area as other creative traditions. The level of education, low exposure of the professions to Black and brown communities, and the difficulties involved in generating the necessary capital to create a building or a landscape are all barriers. Perhaps more importantly, the destruction and "disremembering" of places built by Black people—the environmental analogue to the current era of "whitelash" including the Jim Crow and urban renewal eras—have sparked another theoretical thread associating Black cultural reproduction with nomadic approaches.[9]

Even with Jafa's criticisms, what could BLM's movement—from nonviolent direct action and a focus on "the Black body," to policies affecting communities—mean for designers and planners who work with Black people and Black communities? What are the implications of this era on the landscapes where Black people live, work, worship, remember, and play?

It may be time to not only think about how landscape architecture, as currently constructed, can better serve Black communities, but also about the need to begin a radical rethink of the profession. As the federal government rolls back protections to our rights and resources, how can we rethink our approaches so that Black Landscapes Matter?

For the purposes of this essay, I build from a quote of BLM cofounder Alicia Garza, given at a panel called "Multiracial Movements for Black Lives," sponsored by Race Forward.[10] Ms. Garza identified the underlying motivations for BLM as fighting "to be seen, to live with dignity, and to be connected." I will use these three themes as lenses for viewing landscape situations in the Carolinas in the interest of proposing strategies that offer examples of how Black landscapes (could) matter.

"To Be Seen": They Were Landscape Architects

Slavery and the Design Legacy of Mutuality: Middleton Place, South Carolina

When North and South Carolina were a single colony, Carolina struggled to identify a cash crop to grow that would produce enough profit. Having failed many times, white landowners eventually learned that the climate and tidal action of the rivers surrounding what is now Charleston was ideal for rice production. Plantations, like Middleton Place, were created, but they failed initially for two reasons: one was a lack of local rice-growing knowledge, and the other was exposure to malaria. White plantation owners and their workers were getting sick and dying from malaria in swamp and marsh conditions.

White landowners learned of the Wolof people (then referred to as Senegambians) in present-day West Africa, and of their expertise in rice cultivation.[11] For generations, Wolof people planted, harvested, and processed rice at a large scale. Although called "farmers," Wolof people not only planted and tended crops, but they also perfected intricate lock and flooding systems to maximize rice growth. Additionally, many Wolof people possessed the sickle cell trait. This genetic condition mutates normal disc-shaped red blood cells into sickle shapes, causing chronic clotting, pain, and even death. Even then, doctors knew that the sickle cell trait also produced an increased resistance to malaria. At that time, this characteristic was identified unscientifically and anecdotally, but it aligned with the needs of their slave-based labor practices.

With that knowledge, slave owners specifically plundered West Africa for their rice-farming expertise and strategically bought slaves who were Wolof farmers. During the construction of Middleton Place, fear of malaria resulted in white plantation owners and their white workers spending extended periods downriver in Charleston and away from the plantation. Consequently, Wolof farmers—African people—constructed much of the rice cultivation areas in isolation. Comparing the many characteristics of the rice plantation areas to those in West Africa reveals many similarities, including the indigenous African strain of rice that they cultivated, now known as "Carolina Gold." Its propagation requires planting in wet soils in the "African 'toe-heel' way."[12] Wet soils were used to create dams and dikes designed with wooden gates to allow fresh water to enter and prevent saltwater infiltration; all were nearly identical to systems and structures found in West Africa. And the handmade implements for growing, weeding, harvesting, and processing the rice were also similar to those found across the Atlantic Ocean. They built and, through cross-cultural translation, *designed* the rice-growing plantation and its supportive systems.

For many scholars, the Middleton Place story begins with Henry Middleton's desire to impress white visitors with a dramatic riverfront entry inspired by ideas in Dezallier d'Argenville's *The Theory and Practice of Gardening*. It is most famous for its (former) Main House, sited on a bluff with rippling symmetrical terraces that descend to the main entry, defined by a pair of sculpted "butterfly lakes."[13] It was, however, the success of rice cultivation that led to the wealth that enabled this design and, more broadly, to the economic boom of what is now South Carolina. The formal grounds of Middleton Place were designed by Middleton and implemented by African people, and the cultivated landscape within which the formal grounds operated was designed and built by Africans informed by their indigenous knowledge.

This story arrives at a difficult subject critical to understanding Black landscapes. Slavery in America was one of the most noxious activities in human history. But the narrative suggests that the active selection of skilled African people to build landscapes, including Middleton Place, acknowledged their high level of talent and ingenuity, even under extreme duress. Yet American landscape architecture avoids discussion and recognition of the African and Black contribution to the profession. By any other name, the Wolof people who built Middleton Place, as well as the countless thousands who did similar work across the burgeoning nation, were landscape architects. These Black landscapes were the foundations of wealth and power in this country.

KOFI BOONE

Black Towns

After the end of the Civil War, recently freed Black people endeavored to create their own communities. During Reconstruction, and with newfound access to political and economic power, Black towns and institutions emerged wherever Black people lived. Before the end of the Civil War, Union soldiers defeating Confederate soldiers attracted emancipated Black people, who settled near Union encampments. In 1865, and immediately after the end of the Civil War, at a former encampment situated across from the Town of Tarboro, North Carolina, and within the floodplain of the Tar River, the land was dubbed Freedom Hill. Twenty years later, a Black community elder named Turner Prince purchased the land, and it was renamed Princeville, the first incorporated Black town in America.[14]

Though Princeville may look like other rural towns in eastern North Carolina, it carries significant histories. Shiloh Landing marks the point along the Tar River where enslaved peopled disembarked into brutal lives of forced labor and captivity. Another riverfront site was later accessed by congregants of local churches, arriving in white-robed processions to perform baptismal ceremonies. Princeville, from its infrastructure to its buildings and landscapes, was self-built by Black residents. Many residents were engaged in the timber and mill industries and located their businesses and homes close to the Tar River, built on stilts to help them survive frequent flooding. Powell Park now marks this area and its emotionally charged history—five major floods inundated the town in the twentieth century. Hurricane Matthew ravaged the town in 2016. Princeville's endurance to rebuild in the face of these devastations has made it especially remarkable.

Princeville was socially as well as environmentally vulnerable, due to racism and the sustained threat of white-supremacist violence from nearby communities. Despite these risks, Princeville's population continued to grow, and does so to this day. As an indicator of the place attachment expressed by residents, the town's population increased after the rebuilding periods that followed numerous floods.

Like Princeville, the town of Mound Bayou, Mississippi, also came about by untraditional circumstances. It originated from the enslaved African community of Davis Bend, Mississippi, which was created, in the 1820s, by slave-plantation owner Joseph Davis as a "model" slave community on a plantation. By the standards of America's Peculiar Institution, Davis provided a relatively high level of social, health, and economic care, as well as independence, to Davis Bend's inhabitants. Although still enslaved, residents benefited from dental and health care, opened and ran merchant businesses, and were spared overt domination from overseers. After the Civil War and the collapse of cotton prices, Davis Bend failed, and its residents relocated to the Mississippi Delta bottomlands to found Mound Bayou in 1887. The town earned regional notoriety for its numerous Black owned businesses and organizations, as well as for its tradition of protecting Black people's voting rights amid racial violence. The relative success of the town earned accolades from Booker T. Washington, who called it a model of "thrift and self-government."[15]

Mound Bayou suffered from declining cotton prices and an uptick in Jim Crow–era oppression. The town distinguished itself, however, by providing safe harbor for Black people seeking modest political and economic independence. Serving as a key organizing ground for the Regional Council of Negro Leadership, Mound Bayou attracted interest from prominent civil rights leaders like Medgar Evers. Regional boycotts, in 1952, of service stations and restrooms refusing to serve Black people were organized in Mound Bayou.[16] And, in 1955, the town served as a safe harbor when Black reporters came to Mississippi to cover Emmett Till's murder trial.[17] Mound Bayou continues to exist today, though it grapples with the numerous contemporary challenges facing rural southern towns, including population decline and reduced economic opportunities.

Eatonville, Florida, also founded by Black Americans, in 1887, represents not only the historical significance of free Black towns but also the contemporary roles Black landscape architects can play in their protection and growth. Eatonville emerged from the lack of human rights protections afforded to Black Americans in the post-Reconstruction era. Named after a white landowner, Joseph Eaton, who was willing to sell land to Black people, the town was originally located on just over one hundred acres in what is now known as Greater Orlando.[18] Eatonville was a fully developed town featuring a bustling business district, churches, and one of the largest schools for Black Americans in the region.

Eatonville rose to national recognition due to the writings of one of its most famous residents, Zora Neale Hurston. *Their Eyes Were Watching God,* Hurston's groundbreaking Harlem Renaissance novel presenting unvarnished writing about everyday life in the Black South, was set in Eatonville and other nearby Black towns. Later, Club Eaton was a popular performance and layover spot for a wide array of Black entertainers.[19]

In the late twentieth century, Eatonville was declining, and Orlando's growth was endangering its remaining historic fabric. Everett L. Fly, a Black architect and landscape architect based in San Antonio, Texas, partnered with Eatonville to generate community development guidelines drawing inspiration from Hurston's literary descriptions of the community's character. Furthermore, Fly partnered with Eatonville to launch a Zora Neale Hurston festival. The annual festival extended the visibility of Eatonville's heritage and provided a revenue source to fund future community improvements. In 1988, Eatonville's Historic District was added to the National Register of Historic Places. Eatonville today exists as a town made up of historic pockets intermixed with contemporary development. The town continues to fight for visibility and preservation in the face of Orlando's tourism-driven economic growth.

Princeville, Mound Bayou, and Eatonville reflect the passion and energy of newly emancipated Black people who immediately pursued the creation of places, institutions, and communities. Their cultural landscape legacies still occupy the fringes of the mainstream canons of architecture, landscape architecture, planning, and urban design.

Rosenwald Schools

North Carolina distinguishes itself by having the most Rosenwald Schools in the country. The Rosenwald Fund was born in 1917, after Booker T. Washington, founder of Tuskegee Institute, and Julius Rosenwald, cofounder of Sears, Roebuck and Company, toured the South. Rosenwald, appalled by the deplorable conditions of schools in poor Black rural towns, created the fund to address the disparity between Black and white facilities in the South.[20] It facilitated a collection of school designs and site-plan patterns that prefigured current institutional sustainability issues, including orientation that maximized natural daylight and ventilation, and site planning to enable good sanitation. *Community School Plans,* distributed as a bulletin in 1924, not only addressed the siting and construction of the schools but also recommended landscape and land uses, including the development of adjacent recreation and playground spaces.[21] Additionally, the fund established a matching grant program. If local communities could raise half of the resources required to build a new school, Rosenwald would match it. In many cases, including in Princeville, residents refused the match and raised the entire budget themselves.

Schools in Princeville, Wake Forest, Mount Olive, and many others comprised nearly seven hundred built by Black people across North Carolina.[22] More than five thousand Rosenwald Schools were built across the Southeast. Sadly, many of these sites have fallen into disrepair. But they echo a time when local people—Black people—raised their own funds, contributed their own resources, know-how, and site-planning awareness to hundreds of state-of-the-art facilities in their own communities. They were landscape architects.

Historically Black Colleges and Universities

North Carolina has the most historically Black colleges and universities (HBCUs) of any state. Although largely founded by white philanthropists to prevent Black students from attending predominantly white institutions (PWIs), HBCUs have played and continue to play critical roles in grooming future generations of American citizens. Many campuses were laid out by architects, many of whom were Black Following the lead of Tuskegee Institute, designed by the first Black architect to graduate from a PWI school of architecture (Robert Taylor, from MIT, in 1892), and built by the first generations of students, many HBCUs have vestiges of the community-build model we celebrate today. The people who designed, built, and sustained these campuses during the days of Jim Crow were landscape architects.

The first professionally trained Black landscape architect was David Williston (BS, Cornell University, 1898), a native of Fayetteville, North Carolina. His many accomplishments include, in a twenty-year collaboration with Robert Taylor, Tuskegee University's campus plan, and the campus plan for Howard University.[23] Williston also designed Howard's central gathering space, better known as "The Yard."[24] The import of this space comes largely from the nationally significant events emerging from the buildings bordering the space, including Founders Library, Frederick Douglass Memorial Hall, and Andrew Rankin Memorial Chapel. The Yard and these buildings were the setting that supported two central figures of the modern civil rights movement, Charles Hamilton Houston and Thurgood Marshall. There Marshall formulated the legal cases that led to his victory in the groundbreaking *Brown v. Board of Education* Supreme Court case.[25] Over time, the informal campus quadrangle, edged with large trees, has become a place of celebration and a gathering space for public dialogue. It is also a crossroads, enabling interaction between Black people from across the nation and the campus. For a contemporary understanding of the significance of this space, read Coates's *Between the World and Me,* in which he describes the communality of this space as formative in his own coming of age.

Digging into the origins of the Carolinas and elsewhere, we see that mainstream landscape architecture history, theory, and practice relegates these critical Black landscapes to historic preservation, cultural anthropology, and archeology. Why can they not be read as landscape architecture?

How can one credibly discuss the American landscape without including plantations and the legacy of slavery? This can be a toxic arena, for sure. But with a more nuanced understanding, there are opportunities to reclaim the mutuality that produced the country's earliest landscapes. Enslaved Africans were not big dumb brutes, and white slave owners did not have all of the knowledge and understanding; in the case of a place like Middleton Place, the opposite. Acknowledging this mutuality between Black and white in the midst of such extreme oppression may even reveal alternatives for action in light of the new Jim Crow and addressing the legacy of mass incarceration in contemporary Black communities.

"To Live with Dignity": Public Space for Black Leadership Development

The Negro Park and SNCC

In Raleigh, North Carolina's state capital, open land on the edges of the South Park–East Raleigh neighborhood was purchased through the Works Progress Administration (WPA) and labeled "Negro Park."[26] In part, this designation upheld the Jim Crow legacy of separate but equal facilities for Black and white Americans. Nearby Pullen Park, an amusement park privately donated and funded by the white

Raleigh newspaper owner Stanford Pullen, featured a wide array of amusements but excluded Black people. The "Negro Park" was a part of a larger effort to master-plan a significant section of Raleigh's Black community. The overall plan included not only an amusement park but also a school and public housing. Some local historians consider the "Negro Park" plan one of the first mixed-use master plans in the state. Local Black leaders later successfully petitioned for a name change, and the "Negro Park" became John Chavis Memorial Park. John Chavis lived nearby; he was the first Black teacher allowed to teach both Black and white students in the state.

Within walking distance of Shaw University and St. Augustine's College, the park served as the green heart of Raleigh's Black community. It was also a regional attraction and seen as one of the few "safe places" for Black people traveling between Atlanta and Washington, DC. The who's who of Black political, economic, athletic, and entertainment leaders all frequented the park. Until *Brown v. Board of Education II,* in 1955, its amenities were equal to those in Pullen Park.

The park also supported political organizing. Shaw University is rightfully credited as the home of the Student Non-Violent Coordinating Committee (SNCC), a precedent for BLM, initially led by Ella Baker. South Park–East Raleigh residents alive at that time recall, however, that the initial planning and survival strategies employed in nonviolent direct action were rehearsed in the park. Specifically, the park was home to sessions training Black women to handle threats by aggressive white males in protest action.[27]

The park, and later the university, having grown one of the most important civil rights movements (SNCC), distinguished itself by breaking the patriarchal structure embedded in other organizations, like Dr. King's Southern Christian Leadership Conference (SCLC). SNCC more accurately reflected the roles Black women have historically played in organizing and protest. Acknowledging the role of public space not only in protest action but also in leadership training and development in the Black community is critical to understanding the effectiveness of civil rights–era struggles.

An aside: John Chavis is an ancestor of Ben Chavis, former director of the United Church of Christ's Commission on Racial Justice. Ben Chavis led the development of the report *Toxic Wastes and Race in the United States,* in 1987, the document providing evidence of "environmental racism" and helping to give rise to the environmental justice movement (to be discussed later).

Black Wall Street

Although Oklahoma's Black Wall Street in Tulsa demands full attention in no small part due to its murderous end at the hands of white supremacists, here we will examine another Black Wall Street. Around the same time, in Durham, North Carolina, Parrish Street emerged as the home of what were two of the largest employers of Black Americans in history: North Carolina (NC) Mutual Life Insurance Company, and Mechanics and Farmers (M&F) Bank. At their heights, NC Mutual Life and M&F Bank funded and underwrote more Black land ownership and building construction than any other entities in the country. Their close proximity earned the area the moniker "Black Wall Street."[28] The success of this area extended for generations. Booker T. Washington, W. E. B. Du Bois, Martin Luther King Jr., and Malcolm X all extolled the virtues of what appeared to be the closest example of Black economic self-sufficiency in urban America.[29]

Black Wall Street in Durham was located in the heart of downtown but was inextricably linked to the established Black community of Hayti, southeast of downtown. Hayti surrounded North Carolina (NC) Central University and was the neighborhood of Black Wall Street's business leaders. Equally important, this economic boom provided a "space" for the cultivation of Black political leadership. In addition to the leaders of NC Central University, the Black Wall Street phenomenon led to the emergence of people like Pauli Murray in the mid-twentieth century. Murray, the first Black female Episcopal priest and a queer woman, claimed Durham as her home and base for continued activism and agitation.

The tragedy of Black Wall Street was its location one block from Main Street, or, rather, "White Main Street." The accumulation of this economic influence and political cultivation occurred in the Jim Crow South and was, in a way, regulated by what was known in Durham as the "Gentleman's Agreement." The wealthiest and most powerful white businessmen gave the business leaders of Black Wall Street significant (for the time) influence and decision-making power in the city with one caveat: they did not want to be publicly embarrassed through public protest.

For that reason, there are few records of traditional protest in Durham during the heyday of tobacco and textiles. Conflicts were handled behind closed doors until *Brown v. Board of Education II*. This Supreme Court decision prompted federal mandates for states to eliminate discriminatory practices. Residential desegregation and school integration clashes were among the first breaches of the "Gentleman's Agreement." These events coincided with the decline of textiles and, eventually, tobacco, leading to increased rates of poverty for Black Durham residents that persist today. In the 1960s, the Research Triangle Park (RTP) was proposed as a regional economic development strategy to reposition North Carolina as a national leader in the emerging information and technology sector. Part of the success of the RTP relied upon its connections to the interstate freeway system, and the Durham Freeway was proposed to link the RTP and I-40 to I-85—directly through the Hayti community. Urban renewal, a national planning trend, impacted Durham and Hayti in dramatic ways. With the promise of slum removal and the reinvestment in modern buildings and infrastructure, urban renewal plans for Durham required the demolition of large swaths of the Hayti community, and the elimination of numerous streets that connected it to nearby downtown. The plan was initially accepted by community leaders, but they eventually realized the extent of community destruction it involved. Late protests were unsuccessful. Large areas of Hayti were demolished and replaced with a handful of business and community resources. The promised reinvestment commensurate with what was removed never came to pass. Today, the Durham Freeway is a scar dividing Hayti from downtown, perpetuating grievous generational harm to Durham's Black community.[30]

The contextual success of Black wealth creation and political influence within a white-supremacist system stands as an example of some of the mechanisms designers and planners struggle with today. Namely, where are the local capital reservoirs to draw upon for sustained work in the Black community?

"Creative Protest"

On February 1, 1960, four Black students from North Carolina (NC) A&T State University occupied the lunch counter at Woolworth's in downtown Greensboro, North Carolina. Their sit-in prefigured numerous similar activities across the South and is a key action that launched the modern civil rights movement.[31] Days after the protest, Rev. Dr. Martin Luther King Jr. spoke at White Rock Church in Durham, North Carolina, heralding the student efforts as "creative protest."[32]

The lunch counter eventually integrated, and that action provided a pathway for other college students to find roles in effecting social change. In Durham, students at an ice cream parlor staged a protest similar to the one at the lunch counter. Other protests involved streets. Although these public spaces were not "safe," there was much less flagrant violence than was prevalent in the South at the time. The tenacity of Black students, coupled with hostile but largely nonviolent responses from whites, in part fed North Carolina's past reputation as a moderate part of the South. That moniker no longer applies.

Soul City and the Environmental Justice Movement

In 1969, in an unlikely political alliance, Floyd McKissick, the first Black graduate from UNC Chapel Hill's law school, and longtime leader of the National Association for the Advancement of Colored People (NAACP) and the Congress of Racial Equality (CORE), worked together with President Richard Nixon to develop a "Black New Town" in Warren County, North Carolina.[33] Warren County then ranked, and still ranks, among North Carolina's poorest communities. McKissick, anticipating future regional economic development projects including the Research Triangle Park, saw this new town as a potential industrial and logistics hub in the traditional town pattern where Black residents could live and work in close proximity. Dubbed "Soul City," this effort garnered national attention and design assistance from faculty at North Carolina State University's School of Design.

Soul City was undermined by state and regional lack of cooperation, poor internal organization, and perceptions of impropriety.[34] Homes were built prior to the installment of utilities. Commercial spaces were constructed without pro forma or business plans. Roads were disconnected and, in some cases, pushed to future phases, making the project inaccessible. In the end, the development was shut down partially finished, and it was subsequently used as a tool to discredit all involved. The failure of Soul City is a microcosm of a prevailing attitude toward Black leadership that overlapped with the twilight of Lyndon Johnson's Great Society programs. Not long after the demise of Soul City, Nixon led efforts to divest from community and social programs. This effort, accelerated by Ronald Reagan, permeates contemporary perceptions of Black political leadership as incompetent in cities across the country.

If there is a silver lining to the Soul City story, it is the emergence of the modern environmental justice movement from the same place. In the 1980s, North Carolina was accused of illegally disposing of toxic PCBs in roadside drainage ditches. A court order required the state to remove all PCBs from the ditches and dispose of them in a landfill. The companies involved selected Warren County as the site of this landfill. At the time, it was not revealed that race played an explicit role in site selection. Wealthier white residents in Warrenton (the county seat) helped companies identify places that they thought lacked the capacity for political resistance to the landfill location, and they targeted the Black communities.[35]

As word spread of the proposed landfill siting, former civil rights–era activists, who had not worked since the 1950s and 1960s, and people who were involved in Soul City, mobilized. They deployed nonviolent direct-action tactics, derived from the civil rights movement, for environmental purposes. The protests garnered national attention, including that of academics who were beginning to correlate race and the siting of toxic waste facilities. Ben Chavis, the director of the United Church of Christ's Commission on Racial Justice, was active in these protests, as was Dr. Robert Bullard.

The protests failed, and the landfill was built. However, Chavis's 1987 report *Toxic Wastes and Race in the United States* was groundbreaking. After analyzing Warren County and many other case studies, the report stated that race was the primary determinant in the location of toxic waste facilities, outstripping income and other factors. The researchers said this constituted a pattern of "environmental racism."[36] In addition to the term and methodology, the Warren County protests were recognized as launching one of the first mainstream American environmental movements led by people of color.

As we value the influence of social media and other virtual spaces in organizing, it is important to recognize the power of physical places in developing the many components that effect landscape change. From the role that John Chavis Memorial Park played in nurturing a regional vision of equitable spaces for Black people, to the contributions of Black businesses in building economically self-sufficient Black communities, to the expanded frame of public spaces that include places like lunch counters and college campuses, Black landscapes have encompassed all the places Black people live their lives. Although noble, it is naïve for landscape architects to assume that engaging in the design and planning of public spaces in Black communities addresses merely physical and spatial problems. If public spaces serve more than leisure needs, designers and planners must defend the roles public spaces play in protest action, and join with others skilled in using changes in public space to catalyze political and economic transformation.

"To Be Connected": Relinking Landscape to the Black Creative Ethos

Although heroic efforts have been made to connect landscape architecture with broader arts and culture, divides remain in the perception of landscape's connection to other arts. Ironically, the information age and DIY culture have made access to the tools of making more accessible than ever. Black people are the heaviest users of mobile apps and social media, and they are the most engaged in the production of videos, music, and fashion online. This energy, however, has not impacted the built environment professions, especially landscape architecture. The recent increase in Black graphic and industrial designers illustrates the ability of some Black people to discern the role and value of design when it is connected to the products and experiences we use.

A challenge with the overall topics addressed in this essay is an implicit assumption that, because Black representation is so low in the current profession, interactions between designers and people (a lay public without design training or background) require design expertise on both sides. I have wondered if this attitude and its resultant approaches may have limited the potential for co-creation between designers and Black people. I am struck, all the time, internationally and locally, by the abundance of designing and making in Black communities. I wonder if a more concerted effort to connect Black landscapes with existing Black artists and makers would create new possibilities.

There are some examples where creative lines blur in the process of making culturally significant places. Rick Lowe's work in Project Rowhouses combined the celebration of the John T. Biggers's artistic legacy with the improvisational nature of cultural practitioners working to improve—but not gentrify—the Third Ward of Houston. Theaster Gates's work on the South Side of Chicago blends urban planning, architecture, art, and activism to gather and celebrate Black cultural capital in contemporary ways. When looking at contemporary landscape architecture, one wonders how learning from the dynamic works of contemporary Black artists could inform our creative processes. What could the critical study of and engagement with Lowe and Gates, as well as a Sanford Biggers, Ava DuVernay, Kara Walker, Barry Jenkins, or Solange Knowles, offer in the way of framing the spatial, aesthetic, and experiential qualities of designed places?

Generally, educational training in landscape architecture is devoid of the Black experience. Black educators represent less than 0.5 percent of all landscape architecture educators. Student enrollments have hovered at 1.5 to 2 percent for twenty years. Landscape architecture texts do not reference any contributions by Black landscape architects—no history, theories, case studies, or any other acknowledgments. *Landscape Architecture Magazine* has only recently increased the number of profiles it publishes of Black landscape architects and their works. It is necessary to imagine a future of landscape architecture where there are more pathways to the profession than graduate study. Given the scope of the challenges that we face, that single path seems ridiculously narrow.

It is difficult to attract Black students to the profession when pursuing a degree demands a level of rigor equivalent to other professions with a higher return on investment. It is difficult to do so when our profession offers little in the way of exposing them to Black professionals, projects, history, and theories that reflect them and who they are. As landscape architects, it seems disingenuous to work in Black communities without reflecting deeply on the disconnect between our professional desires and our professional composition. In the face of declining enrollments overall, we must reconsider how and why we teach the next generations about our profession.

Expanding the Canon

If the lack of Black representation is of a piece with declining overall enrollments, a reset is required. What if we told a different story about landscape architecture? Most of our theory, history, and cases apply European precedents to American design challenges. Especially in history and theory courses, we have an implicit professional bias toward not only European landscapes, but privileged European landscapes. One can track European innovations in landscape architecture to their alternating dominance as colonial powers. In some ways, their landscape architecture contributions were funded and created through the domination of other peoples and landscapes. We marvel at the craft but edit the meanings and contexts.

Not even most Europeans enjoyed the use of the landscapes we admire through history and theory. Celebrating the everyday landscapes for the nonpowerful and nonwealthy may send a different message about what landscape architecture may mean to diverse people. Palatial estates were the concretization of monarchies and external symbols of control. Monarchical lands opened to the masses, notably during the Industrial Revolution, were social experiments to "civilize" the working class and maintain control in a capitalist framework. This effort to maintain control, combined with increased ecological awareness, could also describe contemporary design efforts in American cities.

What if there were a *People's History of Landscape Architecture?* Borrowing from Howard Zinn's groundbreaking work *A People's History of the United States,* what if landscape architecture were described with some acknowledgment of the dynamics of race, class, gender, and power?[37] What if it were possible to see yourself in the mainstream of the profession even if you did not aspire to advanced white culture studies? The process of grounding the profession, and therefore the educational foundations, of landscape architecture in the lived experiences of people, including Black people, could make a big difference in its perception and appeal.

Notes

1. Harriet Agerholm, "What Is 'Whitelash,' and Why Are Experts Saying It Led to Donald Trump's Election?," *Independent,* November 9, 2016, www.independent.co.uk/news/world/americas/us-elections/whitelash-what-is-it-white-vote-president-donald-trump-wins-us-election-2016-a7407116.html.

2. Wesley Lowery, "Black Lives Matter: Birth of a Movement," *Guardian,* January 17, 2017, www.theguardian.com/us-news/2017/jan/17/black-lives-matter-birth-of-a-movement.

3. Ta-Nehisi Coates, *Between the World and Me* (New York: Spiegel and Grau, 2015).

4. bell hooks, "Postmodern Blackness," *Post Modern Culture* 1, no. 1 (1990).

5. Craig L. Wilkins, *The Aesthetics of Equity: Notes on Race, Space, Architecture, and Music* (Minneapolis: University of Minnesota Press, 2005).

6. bell hooks, Julie Eizenberg, and Hank Koning, "House, 20 June 1994," in "House Rules," special issue, *Assemblage,* no. 24 (August 1994).

7. Alexandra Sims, "Mannequin Challenge: Black Lives Matter Recreate Police Shootings of Unarmed Black Men," *Independent,* November 11, 2016, www.independent.co.uk/news/world /americas/mannequin-challenge-black-lives-matter-video-police-shootings-philandro-castile -sandra-bland-alton-a7411176.html.

8. Amiri Baraka, *Blues People: Negro Music in White America* (New York: William Morrow, 1960).

9. May Joseph, *Nomadic Identities: The Performance of Citizenship* (Minneapolis: University of Minnesota Press, 1999).

10. "Facing Race: 2019 Program," Race Forward: The Center for Racial Justice Innovation, accessed October 11, 2019, https://facingrace.raceforward.org/program/full-program.

11. Daniel Littlefield, *Rice and Slaves: Ethnicity and the Slave Trade in Colonial South Carolina* (Chicago: University of Chicago Press, 1991).

12. Peter Wood, "'It Was the Negro That Taught Them': A New Look at African Labor in Early South Carolina," *Journal of Asian and African Studies* 9, no. 3–4 (1974): 160–79.

13. "Middleton Place," Cultural Landscape Foundation, https://tclf.org/landscapes/middleton-place#.

14. Joe A. Mobley, "In the Shadow of White Society: Princeville, a Black Town in North Carolina, 1865–1915," *North Carolina Historical Review* 63, no. 3 (July 1986): 340–84.

15. Melissa Block, "Here's What's Become of a Historic All-Black Town in the Mississippi Delta," National Public Radio, March 8, 2017, www.npr.org/2017/03/08/515814287/heres-whats -become-of-a-historic-all-black-town-in-the-mississippi-delta.

16. Peter Brown, "Strike City, Mississippi," *Anarchy* 7, no. 2 (February 1967): 33–37.

17. Olive Arnold Adams, *Time Bomb: Mississippi Exposed and the Full Story of Emmett Till* (Mound Bayou: Mississippi Regional Council of Negro Leadership, 1956).

18. United States Department of the Interior, National Park Service, "National Register of Historic Places Registration Form: Eatonville Historic District" (September 9, 1997), https://np gallery.nps.gov/GetAsset/e5fa60c5-551d-41d3-bbef-2a52ff3a7b0b.

19. United States Department of the Interior, National Park Service, "National Register of Historic Places Registration Form."

20. Stephanie Deutsch, *You Need a Schoolhouse: Booker T. Washington, Julius Rosenwald, and the Building of Schools for the Segregated South* (Evanston, IL: Northwestern University Press, 2011).

21. The Julius Rosenwald Fund, *Community School Plans,* Bulletin no. 3 (Nashville, TN: Julius Rosenwald Fund, 1924).

22. United States Department of the Interior, National Park Service, "The Rosenwald

School Building Program in North Carolina, 1915–1932," in "National Register of Historic Places Documentation Form: Rosenwald Schools in North Carolina, 1915–1932" (July 9, 2015).

23. "Learning from Leaders: David Williston," Tuskegee Institute National Historic Site, National Park Service, last modified February 21, 2018, www.nps.gov/articles/david-williston-learning-from-leaders.htm.

24. Jared Green, "A New Look at the Trail Blazing David Williston," *The Dirt,* August 8, 2016, https://dirt.asla.org/2016/08/08/a-new-look-at-the-trail-blazing-david-a-williston/.

25. United States Department of the Interior, National Park Service, "National Historic Landmark Nomination Form: Andrew Rankin Memorial Chapel, Frederick Douglass Memorial Hall, and Founders Library" (August 2000), www.howard.edu/library/development/Historic LandmarkNom.pdf.

26. Works Progress Administration, "Project Proposal #1 from City of Raleigh," August 14, 1935; Works Progress Administration, Project #65-32-3892.

27. Kofi Boone, "Disembodied Voices, Embodied Places: Mobile Technology, Enabling Discourse, and Interpreting Place," *Landscape and Urban Planning* 142 (August 2015): 235–42.

28. Leslie Brown and Anne Valk, "Black Durham behind the Veil: A Case Study," *OAH Magazine of History* 18, no. 2 (January 2004): 23–27.

29. Sylvia Pfeiffenberger, "Durham's 'Black Wall Street,'" *Duke Today,* January 25, 2007, https://today.duke.edu/2007/01/parrish.html.

30. Andre D. Vann and Beverly Washington Jones, *Durham's Hayti* (Charleston, SC: Arcadia, 1999).

31. William Henry Chafe, *Civilities and Civil Rights: Greensboro, North Carolina, and the Black Struggle for Freedom* (Oxford: Oxford University Press, 1981).

32. Martin Luther King Jr., "A Creative Protest," in *The Papers of Martin Luther King, Jr.,* vol. 5: *Threshold of a New Decade, January 1959–December 1960*, ed. Clayborne Carson et al. (Berkeley: University of California Press, 2005).

33. Christopher Strain, "Soul City, North Carolina: Black Power, Utopia, and the African American Dream," *Journal of African American History* 89, no. 1 (Winter 2004).

34. Strain, "Soul City, North Carolina."

35. Vann R. Newkirk II, "Fighting Environmental Racism in North Carolina," *New Yorker,* January 16, 2016, www.newyorker.com/news/news-desk/fighting-environmental-racism-in-north-carolina.

36. Commission for Racial Justice, United Church of Christ, *Toxic Wastes and Race in the United States: A National Report on the Racial and Socio-Economic Characteristics of Communities with Hazardous Waste Sites* (New York: United Church of Christ, 1987).

37. Howard Zinn, *A People's History of the United States* (New York: Harper and Row, 1980).

THE PARADOXICAL BLACK LANDSCAPE

Trade and Tryon Streets, Charlotte, North Carolina

Walter Hood

For mobile modern man, nostalgia is not so much being uprooted as having to live
in an alien present.
—David Lowenthal, "Past Time, Present Place: Landscape and Memory"

As I stood at the corner of Trade and Tryon Streets in downtown Charlotte, North
Carolina, David Lowenthal's writings on landscape and memory seemed apropos.
Observing the reflective and shimmering buildings, the street furniture and lights,
and the four giant, columnar sculptures placed at each intersection, I was nostalgic.

I grew up in Charlotte in the 1960s and 1970s. It was a different place then, a
city coming into its own in the post–civil rights days. The wards were still intact,
and they gave the downtown spatial clarity; in the First Ward were housing projects; in the Second, civic buildings and space; and in the Third and Fourth Wards,
businesses and light industry.

The crossroads were Trade Street and Tryon Street. As I remember, this was
the place where you saw everyone in Charlotte, Black and white. There were department stores, like Sears and Belk, and smaller establishments like the National

Hat Shop and local appliance shops. It was where we went to the movies and, after, where we waited for our parents to pick us up, at the library.

Standing there, in 2019, I looked for something tangible from that time. As I crossed the street, I noticed a large bronze piece of art, *Il Grande Disco,* a fifteen-foot-diameter sculpture. I immediately approached it and reached out to touch its flat face, trying to push it—something I remembered doing years ago. But it would not move. It was now fixed, immobile.

My past in downtown Charlotte seems irrecoverable to me today. Yet we need the past to understand the present. Maybe, as Lowenthal suggests, the tangible past meets our need for a "diachronic quality of history"—that is, how history has changed and developed over time. *Il Grande Disco*'s immobility is a window to my past in Charlotte. When did it stop moving? Did that even matter to anyone? What had once been "the" piece of art was now clearly a secondary piece of art. It was plainly visible, but cognitively pushed to the side. Like the disc, is this, too, where my memory stops?

Collective Past

When I looked closely at the four giant columns also marking that crossroads, I saw a prospector with a gold pan standing atop one column, a female mill worker on another, an African American with a hammer standing on a third, and, crowning the last column, a mother and child. Created by sculptor Raymond Kaskey, in 1995, the quadripartite sculpture has become a tangible memory in Charlotte's downtown over the last twenty years. But this was not my memory. The descriptive concept by the artist, I read, explained that the piece represented commerce, industry, transportation, and the future. Embodying commerce was the prospector, panning for gold. Maybe it's something I once knew, but this image now had little recall from my lessons in school and from what I remembered in the history books about Charlotte. Industry was evoked by a female mill worker. Here, I was immediately transported back to the Woonsocket Mill, off Monroe Road, where it seemed most of the women and young girls I knew worked. The African American with the hammer depicted transportation—specifically, the making of the railroad, Charlotte's origin story. My only memory of this past from growing up was the folkloric stories of other freed slaves, like John Henry battling a steam engine in the hills of West Virginia. Not to mention that the rail opened in 1856, seven years prior to the Emancipation Proclamation, incontrovertibly indicating who was physically responsible for its existence. The final sculpture, atop the fourth column, of the mother and child signified a universal, homogeneous future. This future was devoid of race in its descriptive imagery. This future was uncontroversial. No one would disagree with it.

Twenty years before the installation of Kaskey's piece, around the time of *Il Grande Disco*'s realization, Charlotte had reflected on its past in a different way. They hired an Italian futurist, Arnaldo Pomodoro, to create a centerpiece celebrating Mecklenburg's independence from the Crown in 1775, the year before the Declaration of Independence. Thus, *Il Grande Disco* was conceived. It represented an abstract future, one that suggested the city's growth radiating out from its center. The giant disc was the first abstract piece of sculpture that I experienced and remember. Its size and mass were heralded at its opening: "Its sheer size (six tons, 15 feet in diameter) suggests a great strength. . . . The fact that the disc will swivel at the touch of a hand or a change in wind direction seems to symbolize the changing moods, responses and independence of a changing, dynamic city."[1] Today, it looks like something from *Star Wars*. But it is the past that I know, one of changing eras, where representation and the limitations of class and race were disappearing. That's what I remember: the newness of this abstract piece of sculpture, amid old buildings and new ones, as proscenium.

As Thomas Wolfe so famously wrote, "You can't go home again." This statement rang true when I stood there at Trade and Tryon (as did the irony that Wolfe, too, was a North Carolina native). But maybe there is a way to return, by understanding the altered and the tangible. What if the Pomodoro piece had been built in 1995, and the Kaskey piece in 1975, or, more importantly, could they have been? Today, in contemporary art by African Americans, the Black image has emerged as an instigator rather than as a celebratory rouse. In 2005, in Indianapolis, when the artist Fred Wilson attempted to sculpt a Black image from the past by copying and liberating a freed slave from an obelisk in the city's center, the Black community objected. They instead wanted to see themselves represented in a way that considered the current Black experience. Kara Walker's three-dimensional cutouts echo the Blackness of James Marshall's mundane and everyday representations of Black life, but hers evince the darkness, violence, and perversity to which Black lives were often subjected. Kehinde Wiley's equestrian statue *Rumors of War* intrepidly occupies its resting place in Richmond, Virginia, where it endeavors to shift the city's historical narrative. My own project, Witness Walls, in Nashville, Tennessee, illustrates police violence as well as Black reserve—images of ordinary Black people on eight-foot concrete panels depict extraordinary acts of passive resistance.

These currents counter the erasure of Blackness in America's urban environment. Like the sculptures at Trade and Tryon, these representations suggest that we all collectively fear losing our identity in space and place.

Denying, Remaking, and Inventing an Ostensible Past

When examining Charlotte's demographic profile as described by census data from 1970 to 2010, I was surprised to learn of its racial makeup. When I was growing up, African Americans comprised about a third of the city's census count. By the 1990s, Blacks' numbers had increased to almost half the population, and, now, together with an increasing Latino population, constitute just under 50 percent. In the 1970s, Blacks were subordinate in number to Charlotte's white population.[2] Maybe this was why we could—why we were allowed to—mix in places like Trade and Tryon. The places we ventured to outside of the neighborhood were white landscapes that we navigated carefully. Even though my early childhood years were lived in a segregated South, it seemed integrated. Blacks' nonthreatening, subservient existence in the public realm has a long history in the landscape of the American South; it was the Black landscape I came to know—and one in which I was always a second-class citizen. Like most of us reflecting on the past, when I look back on it now, it seems strangely romantic—if fraught with the segregative regulations that determined the actions and expectations of citizens in the public realm.

When the Charlotte census reflected a larger African American population, Black landscapes began to shape the city's image. These were not the same segregated Jim Crow landscapes of the earlier years. In these landscapes, the Black body in space symbolized something different. I remember reading about Charlotte's rise in crime, in the early 1990s, as the crack epidemic ravaged the city's Black neighborhoods. These landscapes quickly became ghettos as disinvestment followed the flight of the Black middle class. Leaving one group of people—the lower-income people—to sustain themselves without the resources of a more economically diverse community is the predicament of the dynamic Black landscape. The housing projects of the mid-twentieth century were never intended as permanent housing and neighborhoods. They were temporary quarters, places where you could "get on your feet" and "pull yourself up by the bootstraps." It was the place where you saved in order to one day purchase a house. My father and mother worked multiple jobs, day and night, to save for the down payment that moved us from Statesville Avenue to Druid Hills. That was the process. I remember during and after the Vietnam War, in the early 1970s, Black families moved to Druid Hills from the Statesville Avenue projects. Black families, using the GI Bill to purchase homes, were participating in the American dream.

But the American dream was doomed from the beginning—that's one paradox that has plagued Black landscapes. Chasing the American dream may as well have been chasing the carrot. This passage, describing Charlotte, describes the impossibility of realizing the dream:

> As early as 1910, discrete black and white areas were created across the four wards that formed the city. Ultimately, it was the federal government's New Deal programs that gave impetus and financial resources to support racial discrimination of Charlotte-Mecklenburg's African-American community. Starting in the 1930s, segregation by race was sanctioned in the New Deal's backing of low-cost mortgages and refinance loans to promote and preserve white homeownership. For white families, who thrived from decades of accrued wealth benefits, these programs spurred one of the largest accumulations of wealth in our country's history. But the same cannot be said for families of color. Federal "red lining" prohibited them from getting loans to buy a home. All neighborhoods where the majority of residents were people of color received the bottom rating for investment. Even middle-class African-American neighborhoods were ranked at the bottom.[3]

This transitory, dynamic, and unsustainable paradox makes easy the erasure and re-invention of Black landscapes. In this suburban Charlotte where white flight had moved beyond the city periphery, the new banking capital saw problems with this visual dichotomy. I remember when they moved the bus lines, in the 1990s, from Trade and Tryon Streets to a new route away from Independence Square, making way for the novel, ostensible past to emerge. Maybe Charlotte did not want to become Atlanta, or Washington, DC—the "Chocolate City." Instead, it chose to leap back to a more romantic memory, not to the abstract, promise-filled modern time that Pomodoro had depicted in his piece, fueled by the civil rights movement and the rich idea of integration. In Pomodoro's modern era, new homes could have been built downtown in the First Ward for the then-diverse community, instead of relocating them. A transit mall on Trade and Tryon could have been established to celebrate the city's working class. Charlotte could have integrated the areas not redlined, adding diversity to neighborhoods like Myers Park and Freedom Park. Instead, the ostensible past emerged on the four corners of Independence Square, and the Black representation was that of a (freed) slave with a hammer.

Altered and Tangible Past

Charlotte's Black landscapes are diachronic. The changes along Trade and Tryon are emblematic of the transformation that has altered the city's memory of Black landscapes. What's left is a tangible past, one that reflects the evolution of the redlined city, in places like Druid Hills, Double Oaks, and Beatties Ford Road—the neighborhoods where only Blacks could live. Like the First Ward, these were Black landscapes. The redlined and racially segregated city created Black landscapes where we all lived, no matter our social status, class, or religious faith. I had friends who went to Catholic school, others to public school. We all mixed because we had to. There were upper-class families, middle-class families, and lower-class families all together. You could read in the landscape the upward mobility route of Black families. We lived in Double Oaks before moving to Druid Hills. We never got to Beatties Ford Road, the landscape of the upper-class Black families in West Charlotte, because by the time my family could afford a bigger house, the first ring of white suburbs was accessible to us. We later left Druid Hills for Hidden Valley. Then, no one knew that in twenty years we'd create another Black landscape.

This is the paradox the Black family grappled with as segregation gave way to integration, and as they gained access to other parts of the city. The public housing projects of Double Oaks, and the single-family working- and middle-class neighborhood of Druid Hills, are now distant memories. But, in my memory—and, I imagine, in the memories of most Blacks raised in Charlotte during the 1960s and 1970s—the segregated neighborhood represents the seminal Black landscape, even though it contradicts our collective memory of change and progress. Paradoxically, it is this collective memory that makes the ostensible past possible.

The Irrecoverable Past

The paradox of the Black landscape in the urban United States is that although its physicality has been erased, it lives in the collective consciousness of American society as a mnemonic device. It has created a mystic of cool through its marginalized and subservient existence. It's a place that is mythical and seems to always live in the past. The Black landscapes are lived experiences. They aren't only mythical; they are real—and the culture we know from those landscapes haunts our memories. I am nostalgic for those separate but equal times. Growing up in a neighborhood with teachers, doctors, lawyers, insurance salesman, and librarians alongside plumbers, butchers, mechanics, store managers, and garbage collectors was common in Druid Hills. In my memory, community seemed sustainable. Today, we can only imagine a landscape like that.

On a recent trip to Charlotte, I wondered if Price's Chicken Coop still existed. My mother would pick up fried chicken sandwiches there on her way home from work at the Uniform Rental plant. Now, I drove through a foreign landscape that I did not remember. In the distance, Price's brick building came into view. It seemed old and out of place among the new condominium and retail spaces. I pulled into a parking lot behind the brick building. Outside, groups of young white people had gathered, eating chicken and talking.

When I entered Price's, I was home again. Seeing the Black men and women behind the counter, and the line out of the door made me smile. The crowd was diverse—young white hipsters mixed with Black customers. We ordered sandwiches and sat across the street on a grassy slope adjacent to the light-rail line. As I sat there eating the sandwich, my taste buds had definitely arrived home. But as I looked around, I had to admit that I had entered an alien future.

Notes

1. Maria David, "1974: Welcome to Uptown Charlotte's 'Great Disc,'" *Charlotte Observer,* updated August 16, 2015, www.charlotteobserver.com/news/local/article31203281.html.

2. "U.S. Decennial Census," *Social Explorer,* https://socialexplorer.com/explore-tables.

3. Leading on Opportunity, "Chapter 2: The Impact of Segregation," Opportunity Task Force Report, www.leadingonopportunity.org/report/chapter-2.

A TALE OF THE LANDSCAPE

Detroit, Michigan

Maurice Cox

When I started as director of the City of Detroit Planning and Development Department (PDD) in the spring of 2015, the popular narrative surrounding this midwestern city was that it epitomized postindustrial malaise, with the effects of disinvestment and neglect starkly etched across the environment. Working closely with residents of this city, however, I found a more positive and complex paradigm in which challenges became moments of transformative opportunity.

Detroit is a dynamic city, with a population that demonstrates creativity and innovation infused with a strength and resilience coming from centuries of resistance, self-determination, and a refusal to quit. The invention of Motown music, for which Detroit is known, emerged from the same resolve and creativity that has consistently characterized African American artistic expression. The American dream of single-family home ownership, also born in Detroit, drove Black people as well as white people to strive for a better future and reap the rewards of middle-class opportunity. During the years of disinvestment, these same people found their own resources to overcome administrative budget deficiencies and insolvency.

In 2015, under Mayor Mike Duggan's administration, city planning was charged with acknowledging and supporting those who had remained in Detroit while others fled to the suburbs in search of opportunity. Today, with a population that is over 80 percent African American, Detroit is one of the largest majority Black cities in the United States. Considering the history of injustice this people has experienced in this country, we as planners have a responsibility and an opportunity to try to set things right as much as possible. Disinvestment and abandonment resulted in thousands of vacant buildings and, following their subsequent demolition, in swaths of vacant land. With slogans such as Black Lives Matter dominating the national political airwaves, here in Detroit the public administration and the PDD committed to acknowledging that Black landscapes matter.

To frame my position and approach to the work in Detroit, I will begin by sharing the context of some earlier chapters in my career. I was born and educated in New York City, then spent ten years in Florence, Italy, and seventeen years in Charlottesville, Virginia. The Metropolitan City of Florence has a typical European cultural urban form and civic realm. The relationship between built and natural forms is clearly delineated; the countryside is the countryside, and the city is the city. In Charlottesville, Virginia, I encountered a different reality that stood in stark contrast to the one in Florence. Rural and urban forms were interwoven. Landscape forms physically structured urban form, a circumstance that deeply influenced the thinking of the intellectual and architectural designer Thomas Jefferson. Indelibly printed on the local landscape, his works and thoughts began to resonate with me. Jefferson recognized that "design activity and political thought are indivisible" and often subtly manifest in landscape form. An example of Jefferson employing this approach is the design of the University of Virginia, where the form of the Lawn, surrounded and embraced by the buildings intended for faculty and teaching, represents the commons, a space imbued with freedom of interaction, education, and democracy.

The relationships in Virginia between landscape and building, and between academic and vernacular, contrasted sharply with what I had seen in Europe and critically influenced my development as an urban planner. It was through this experience that I came to understand the tendency of the American landscape to erase certain aspects of history. Specifically, those in power iteratively eroded the social and cultural signs, in the form of schools and churches of low-income immigrant and African American communities, until mere fragments remained within the larger urban landscape. Acknowledging such erasure led me to realize that I was a preservationist and that I needed to act on a prevalent attitude. To bolster this ideological position, I engaged in the organization of my community to understand how form, inherent in these buildings and their landscapes, conveyed culture, if only we knew how to read it. My own house in Charlottesville at 702 Ridge Street—a historic American four-square from the late nineteenth century—existed in a landscape among other, more vernacular, buildings. Yet, despite the presence of buildings such as mine, the neighborhood was neither protected nor revered, and, as president of the Ridge Street Neighborhood Association, I began to question why.

In Charlottesville, if you look only at the high, or academic, architecture, you miss part of the story. The history of people of color in these neighborhoods tends to unfold in modest everyday architecture, so in order to understand one part of the neighborhood, you must engage the other. This engagement involves the stories of people. In other words, buildings are part of a cultural landscape that knits together the land, the people, and their stories. As a developing historic preservationist, I learned that if I wanted to respect my neighbors, my discussion of historic structures had to consider the street's humble residential spaces. Here, these included the Nimo House, built and owned by an African American, or the cottage in which a slave cabin was embedded. It was through acknowledging these kinds of everyday buildings that I began to understand the reciprocity that exists between them and the land on which they were built.

Studying the landscape further revealed a series of hierarchies and patterns reflecting notions of property ownership, issues of segregation and marginalization, and the role of land characteristics such as topography in deploying or reinforcing these hierarchies. Ridge Street, for example, took its name from the landform on which the homes in my neighborhood were built. This landform then bound the buildings into a narrative about culture and society. At the crest of the ridge stood the substantial stylistic homes typically built for white people, and at the base of the ridge, and at its head and tail, were the more modest and fragile structures African Americans owned. The land tied the buildings into a neighborhood, and its natural features framed a specific social narrative, yet only by more closely examining the modest buildings did an alternative narrative, equally deserving of attention, become clear.

In reexamining the significance of everyday buildings and landscapes, the question arises of who should care for these sites. Who should steward these less visible spaces, and who should preserve these communities? Inevitably, those who do preserve them are the inhabitants who have lived their stories. They are people of color, and, in their attempts to keep these places vital through maintenance and care, they have unconsciously performed the function of the preservationist.

Moving more deeply into the context of rural Virginia, I came to know Bayview, a low-income, African American rural community in Northampton County. Bayview's residents understood the cultural resonance of the land and desired to work with and impact it. Alice Coles, a local community organizer, introduced me to the South African slogan, "Nothing about us, without us, is for us." Bayview, as I discovered, was a proud community living in absolute poverty, lacking access to clean drinking water and indoor plumbing. Nevertheless, this community had a deep understanding of their historic cultural ties to the land. This was a rural culture embedded in the substandard houses they inhabited.

Our job as designers envisioning a new Bayview village was to interpret those homes and somehow preserve the essence of that cultural identity. In order to do this community justice and give the residents the respect they deserved, patience was imperative; the project took six years to complete. Over time, we developed an understanding of this complex rural village character and the extent of its history, which reached back to the enslaved and free people who worked the land. This was a community of folks who were born of a long history of farmers, and they wanted their new rural village to be interpreted as the result of a precise relationship between settlement and farmland. The idea of an agricultural practice backing right up to the kitchen door was identified as the long-established model that continued to exist. This insistence on the continuity of culture proved an important lesson for me.

More lessons came when I moved to New Orleans several years after Hurricane Katrina had devastated the city. There I encountered a people with the universal desire to heal communities of color by encouraging self-determination. They demanded the appropriate support from the government and called on all to engage a process of imagination, accountability, and building. "Building" addressed existing structures that were often labeled blight. Their concern, I understood, was legitimate. My knowledge of the negative effect urban renewal has had on cities, particularly in minority communities, made me seriously suspicious of the label "blight" that has been attached to modest buildings in the local urban fabric. I knew that these buildings had cultural narratives embedded within them, yet they were the most vulnerable to the demolition schedule.

The people of New Orleans were fiercely protective of their heritage and wanted to control the organizational and design energy directed at their city post-Katrina. They also wanted to author new design in their communities. They had seen too much of their culture worn away through blanket dismissal of the social and cultural narratives typically hidden in cinder-block buildings—buildings that could easily have witnessed the early performance of jazz or other genres of African American music, for instance. My staff and students at the City Center, an arm of Tulane University School of Architecture, worked from the premise that such erasure should be avoided at all costs. We intentionally tackled projects that sought to adaptively reuse these modest structures and preserve their historic cultural narratives.

One such project was the Dew Drop Inn on LaSalle Street in the Mid-City neighborhood. The Inn had once combined two wood-frame houses into a performance space, bar, and hotel and offered some of the great early twentieth-century jazz musicians a space to entertain and relax afterward. In the late twentieth century, when the buildings had lost their original use and fallen into disrepair, presenting an image of dilapidation yet retaining cultural significance, the question of how to attract new interest, encourage reuse of the space, and create awareness of the site's historic significance—in a way, "tagging" it—was imperative. This so-called blighted property had a richness that belied its impoverished state; it simply needed some care and attention. First, we influenced the capital fundraising campaign for the site's redevelopment by creating a pop-up with a mural that depicted Dew Drop Inn performers. By literally plastering the facade with images of the activities that had created the site's cultural landscape, we drew attention to its former vibrancy and significance.

I'm also fond of a collaborative project I worked on with the New Orleans Mardi Gras Tribal Council. This group of African American men gather in secret to sew the elaborate sequined and feather-embellished suits for their annual ritualistic

Super Sunday event—a performance distinct from the citywide Mardi Gras parade. Traditionally, the performance acts out the clashing of competing tribes in a mock street fight, which unfolds through dancing and chanting into a public festival. The men do most of the sewing, passing on the tradition to their family members; women participate in the parade and in the tribal councils as queens to the tribal chiefs. Most important, however, is that this secret culture occurs behind the closed doors of domestic space until the moment the suits are revealed in public. As soon as the Mardi Gras celebrations end, the costumes are disassembled until the making process begins anew the following year. The ritualistic dance performance, a fleeting, intangible activity, occurs in the street, so public space becomes the site of occupation.

These intensely ephemeral practices render the Mardi Gras Indian tradition fragile, and international scrutiny directed at New Orleans, post–Hurricane Katrina, compounded this fragility as the Mardi Gras Indians found their imagery appropriated by mainstream culture. As a result, the Mardi Gras Indian community wondered how they might drive economic development to further their local cultures, and what possibilities might exist for the long-term transfer of their culture from one generation to the next.

The question of rendering LaSalle Street as a cultural artifact and preparing it for reinvestment also became imperative, as did the need to improve the relationship between the street and the buildings within which the sewing occurred. The City Center designed and built a giant porch across the facade of two shotgun houses purchased by the tribes, creating a stage in an interstitial space between the inside and outside. But how to envision an entire street marked by the Mardi Gras Indians' presence? After a series of studies, we assisted the tribes' investment in the open space of the street. By claiming it, they became community developers, focusing on the significance of the street and property. The Mardi Gras Indians purchased the entire neighborhood block and aggregated diverse projects for the greatest impact. They preserved a stand-alone shotgun house and a separate group of shotgun houses with their adjacent vacant properties, all of which face A. L. Davis Park and now form the nucleus of a Mardi Gras Indian campus. This preservation development strategy has given full agency to the men who, in the months leading up to the Mardi Gras festival, convene weekly to sew their elaborate suits. Now they have taken charge of the street where their rituals play out, and thus have greater control of its future development.

Now I arrive at this essay's focus, the city of Detroit. While in Detroit, I have developed strong collaborative relationships with the academy, the philanthropic community, and residents in trying to reimagine the city. Despite its widely disseminated image as a city in ruins, Detroit still matters for many reasons. It matters because it is one of the largest African American–majority cities in America. It is also one of the largest cities in America, at 139 square miles in area. It matters for cultural reasons as the birthplace of several American music genres, as the site of modern automobile manufacturing and its resultant lifestyle, and as the place where iconic athletes, such as Joe Lewis, started their careers. Detroit is a vast cultural landscape, especially with regard to African American heritage, but it is in dire need of care.

There is still much to be done in Detroit to revitalize its vast and beautiful urban landscape. Though I could share many of the approaches to revitalization I availed myself of during my tenure as PDD's director, here I focus on the productive city and the regenerative power of landscapes. Returning for a moment to the history of this city as the birthplace of various genres of music, and specifically Motown, I want to refer to native-Detroiter Marvin Gaye's famous song "Mercy Mercy Me." Many may not know that the song's alias was "The Ecology," penned in 1971, when Motown, in Detroit, was transitioning to a more socially conscious sound. Even in the cultural milieu of the city, "The Ecology" became a rallying cry—an anthem of sorts—that emanated from an industrial landscape, lamenting the global damage done by universal failings to control the emission of pollutants.

During this time, Detroit epitomized the condition of a failed or obsolete industrial system, suffering a 60 percent decline in population that left behind vacant homes, vacant land, an acutely disinvested infrastructure, and a demographic of which 36 percent lived below the poverty line. Detroit in the 1970s was a city in deep distress. The population flight left majestic theaters without audiences, ballrooms without dancers, and schools without a purpose. The city that invented modern manufacturing had become obsolete, and, by the early 2000s, Detroit was renowned as a failed city with the largest documented bankruptcy in American history. National headlines expressed such an overwhelmingly negative narrative that it took hold of our collective imagination as we observed with morbid fascination a once-great American city teeter on the brink of death. This is the Detroit that many have come to know: a place characterized by staggering negative statistics. Even after removing eighteen billion dollars of debt, only about 40 percent of the city's streetlights were illuminated at night. Nevertheless, during the toughest times, a unique kind of determination and stubbornness developed among those who remained, producing a collective culture of Detroit versus everybody else. The population somehow sustained itself through a historical support system accustomed to self-reliance.

While the prevailing narrative conjured images of an ecological nightmare, it is helpful to remember that cities themselves are ecological systems. They expand, they contract, they adapt, they resist. What endures in Detroit is resilience—a refusal to quit—that comes from a grit and determination that made Detroit rise as the locus of the American dream. Its population of over 1.9 million comprised waves of individuals flooding into Detroit during the Great Migration from the American South and aspiring, through their labor, to build a better, richer, fuller way of life. These individuals effectively built the middle class. They created cultural icons and established another narrative that we associate with more prosperous, optimistic times when music was one of several dominant cultural resources spreading Detroit's fame across the globe. Its population climbed the ladder of wealth produced by the American obsession with the automobile.

The fabric of neighborhoods where people purchased single-family homes continues to exist in multiple iterations across the city, allowing us to imagine the future potential of Detroit. Many of these neighborhoods were places where African Americans were forbidden residency due to official local and state redlining. Today, African Americans from across the social spectrum and from all walks of life populate every one of these neighborhoods, even neighborhoods such as Lafayette Park, designed by the famed modernist architect Mies van der Rohe.

Detroit today, with a population of about seven hundred thousand, is at a tipping point. New cultural landscapes are being created as the city experiences a resurgence that brings about strange juxtapositions, such as the large groups of Black men gathering to play basketball in the downtown public space of Cadillac Square, or the mutual urbanite and suburbanite claim to the city that occurs during the now famous "Slow Roll." Slogans such as "Nothing Stops Detroit" reverberate across downtown, representing the manifestation of the revived and vigorously beating heart of the city.

The sites where the PDD has been charged to work, however, are where the soul of the city resides: in its neighborhoods. In the words of James Brown, the population of Detroit is "ready for the big payback." Pivoting away from downtown also acknowledges that neighborhoods are the places where innovation will reemerge. The challenge is to concede the value of what is already there, and to keep the people who remained in place—those who resisted the lure of the suburbs or places with greater economic potential. These are the folks who are planning to stay, and it is our job to make a place for them and to finally grant them a return on their investment. These are the folks who have taken care of their neighborhoods; they mow the grass of vacated lots and maintain the homes that have, by necessity, been abandoned. These are the folks who, over the years, continue to sustain the city, preserving the urban landscape through the tools of their trade and the skills they developed while previously employed in the blue-collar jobs of the automobile industry. Often, such tradespeople are also artists: culture bearers who once built cars and now build Shinola bikes.

The new payback supports and reinvigorates places where these people can gather and meet on a Saturday, places like Eastern Market, one of the most diverse in the city. The payback includes the millennial generation, the young people who were born and raised in Detroit, left for college, and return now to be a part of their city's comeback story. Fundamentally, this payback is the democratization of design whereby folks are mobilized to tackle enormous challenges. The democratization of design happens in a way that shares the burden and responsibility of seeking answers and solutions, allowing new design and planning to emanate from the residents' own values—and not ours as city officials and design professionals.

Detroit is an expansive city encompassing the combined size of the cities of San Francisco, Boston, and Manhattan within its 139 square miles. Vacancy alone totals an area about the size of Manhattan. How does a planning department work with such figures, and how does that translate into a discussion about design? When I arrived in Detroit, I inherited one planner for every 138,000 residents, given its population of about 690,000 people. For a city of 139 square miles, that's one planner for every twenty-nine square miles of the city.

As my first professional task in Detroit, I made a value proposition for planning and design. I restructured the planning department and created three citywide divisions: the Office of Zoning Innovation; the Office of Arts, Culture and Entrepreneurship; and an office of "Yes" (as opposed to "No, we cannot do this") that was to manage our philanthropic and higher education partnerships. This new effort also attempted to create one of the most diverse planning departments in the country. Sixty percent of the staff were people of color, 55 percent of the women were in leadership positions, about 30 percent were from Michigan, and in total about twelve languages were spoken. I hired about twenty-five new planners, but only five were professionally trained as city planners; five were landscape architects, five were architectural historians, five were architects, and five were urban designers. They work in interdisciplinary teams, and at the core of their responsibilities is the imperative to engage at all scales of the community. The engagement is crucial to reestablishing an atmosphere in which people can trust us to build an inclusionary growth scenario, where economic opportunity exists for all, and where trust and planning can be reestablished. Leading the effort is Mayor Duggan, Detroit's first white mayor in thirty years, whose dream is to preside over the regrowth of the city and witness its first population increase in his lifetime. In line with this goal, the aim is to retain the existing population and create a quality of life that is so high that it also attracts new residents.

A characteristic of the failed city that was once seen as a negative element in Detroit's urban condition—a surplus of vacant land—now works to our competitive advantage. Is it possible to transform this fallow land into a force that drives revitalization? Is it possible to do so in ways that allow longtime residents to become equity investors? What might it mean to create a productive landscape such as an orchard in a neighborhood? To own the orchard or the grove of trees beside your house? How might we implement new models of collective ownership? The stakes were high as the bar was already set by the planning work of the nonprofit organization Detroit Future Cities (DFC), undertaken in 2012. Changing the conversation in Detroit from the simple question of *how do we grow again,* DFC asked, *how can we become an incredible, world-class city of seven hundred thousand residents?* They were the first to question what should be done with these assets and who should plan the city. By engaging tens of thousands of people in that conversation, they set the bar high, and we are proceeding from that point forward.

Visualizing the vacant land in a series of DFC-produced diagrams helped us realize that certain parcels could be put to productive use, but first we had to change the dialogue about vacancy. Diagrams visually portray land through demarking and color-coding, but such methods can cause controversy because embedded in the color-coded green areas are tens of thousands of people who live in a rural-like setting mere minutes from downtown. Our charge is to rationalize and make sense of it while increasing the well-being of the current residents.

I have searched nationally and internationally for models that might provide answers to these questions, examples that represent a transformation of land that drives new development with an ecological agenda. Have there been approaches that merge performative landscapes with green infrastructure? Or strategies that re-use open space in formerly industrial landscapes for public access, such as greenways like the Dequindre Cut, an unused rail line repurposed for pedestrian and bicycle access to the river? How could we take that framework a step further, transforming land adjacent to those greenways to drive revitalization inclusive of medium-density housing currently lacking in the city? Could this relatively short and local riverwalk greenway expand to link to an inner-circle greenway that loops around the city all the way from Eight Mile (the street that forms the northernmost boundary of the city limits) and back down to the river, in an off-road pathway?

The PDD is also exploring whether vacant lots could create a renewable energy economy, functioning similarly to Walter Hood's Solar Strand at the University of Buffalo. In the spring of 2018, ten acres of vacant land received one of the largest collections of solar arrays ever installed in an urban neighborhood. The project gives back to the community by redesigning adjacent parcels of land into a four-acre park. The possible repurposing of a recreation center at the site reuses architectural elements to build an observation platform and creates a focal point for the park where residents and visitors can interact with the science and technology of the solar array.

During the years of extreme disinvestment and poverty in the city, many residents grew produce in vacant lots, establishing the urban agriculture for which the city has become known. Citizens of similar postindustrial cities aspire to adopt a large-scale urban agriculture model as part of the new economy. In Detroit, we wondered about the specific form this might take, such as formalizing a close-knit relationship between neighborhood agriculture and nearby development. Maintenance is paramount when considering agricultural interventions on vacant lots, and strategies must be developed to support a low-maintenance regime. The regime would not be zero-maintenance, but one that is manageable long-term without the encumbrance of added expense. The intention crafts a typology of landscapes, whether tree nurseries, agricultural, or other such efforts. In all cases, the proposition implies that landscape can constitute a form of urbanism that begins to structure urban development.

Many of the models I have discovered tend to be of a utopian nature, and I am trying to understand how such strategies might be applied to Detroit's context. One strategy that comes to mind is Marshall Brown's Smooth Growth® plan in Chicago, which operates on a no-growth principle. The land is charged with a different role: the urban grid is overlaid with a softer system of land stewardship and land formation, with public and private zones fluidly interwoven to form a type of twenty-first-century garden city. Other strategies include those in municipalities with similar conditions, such as Baltimore, where vacant land is repurposed to create parks and gardens as well as urban farms; Atlanta, where a twenty-two-mile greenway loop has transformed the relationship between a series of neighborhoods; and Philadelphia, where one goal is to reshape five hundred acres of underutilized land into parks.

Whatever the model, it must make sense while providing a theory that fits the practical application of a strategy. One theory that seems appropriate is the notion of the city within the city, in which hyperdense urban areas exist like an archipelago in a system of green spaces. After examining a 2004 PDD figure-ground drawing depicting the downtown core as represented by Detroit Future City, with its plethora of vacant land, I felt it important that those open spaces should not be rebuilt but should instead remain as intentional landscapes.

When I became the planning director, I revisited that DFC diagram showing vacant land. I focused on the places where people live, the most populated places with their beautiful tree-lined streets and lawns in front of single-family homes. Detroit has a multitude of these geographies, which raised the question of how to knit together, like a quilt, the interstitial land. In some areas of the city, a wilder type of landscape could juxtapose with urban productive landscapes. The latter could co-exist with residential space, and with purposeful greenways connecting portions of one island village to another active space. Other spaces could exist simply as natural areas.

As I mentioned above, our goal was to create an overarching strategy based on a typology of landscape forms. A diagram could illustrate areas where density could be increased, as well as areas intended to serve as connective tissue. Other future landscapes include Rouge River Park on the west side of the city, which will focus on a biodiverse naturalistic landscape that links open green spaces and existing parks; the Inner Circle Greenway, which ties all of the neighborhoods together like charms on a bracelet; and the Iron Belt Line, which continues from the riverfront up into the neighborhoods. We assembled interdisciplinary teams to dig deeper into the possibilities of these landscapes. Eventually, a vision of how these elements might connect started to emerge.

Perhaps the city's most significant landscape planning strategy is at the water-front, which forms an international border between the United States and Canada. It's challenging to create a riverfront like no other American city has created: one where everyone is welcome, and not only to recreate but to live. Detroit's extraordi-nary riverfront is one of the most diverse I have ever seen, both as a cross-section of the region and considering the population that comes together here. The planning strategy should reflect this diversity.

To create a place that welcomes everyone, we began with a process that was equally inclusive in terms of engagement. Over a six-month period, we engaged the public in multiple ways, from boat rides to bike rides, walks, and group meetings. We believed that the public could learn along with the jury, and we opened the doors to the selection process, admitting about two hundred people who observed presentations by six multidisciplinary teams. The commission winners, SOM with French landscape architect Michel Desvigne, were asked to construct heightened density and create distinct neighborhoods along a two-mile stretch of the river while also reclaiming the landscape as public space. This process was the result of a thirty-year vision and about twenty million square feet of new development, includ-ing a series of twenty-minute walkable neighborhoods stretching from Heart Plaza to Belle Isle. The strategies can be understood in parts: neighborhood parks and greenways that provide the connective tissue between the neighborhoods; streetscape and public realm improvements; mixed-used commercial corridor redevelopment; and single-family stabilization through rehab.

Ten years ago, the riverfront was dominated by cars and parking garages. The best view of the river was from your car on the eighth floor of a parking structure. Today at the riverfront, an ecologically vibrant landscape has become part of a continuous promenade. Stormwater management occurs within a wetland park. Many parcels originally bid out for private development have transitioned into public space, allowing citizens to fish, stroll, bike, and enjoy the views along the pier. This planning framework has helped create a highly democratic landscape with development pushed to the edges. Further interventions include new lighting, paving, and seating along the fingers of smaller greenways that weave through a series of cooperatives and low-income housing developments that, though historically lacking access to the river, now can be connected.

Regenerating neighborhoods in Detroit is part of the payback ethos that we as a planning department attempt to honor. A final example will occur in the Livernois/McNichols neighborhood on the northwest side of Detroit. Here, community identity and pride remain strong, yet many of the homes have foreclosed, with approximately four hundred lots and one hundred houses in public ownership. We searched for a strategy to break down the scale of neighborhood blocks, two thousand feet in length, while resolving the issue of vacant lots. We developed a typology of landscapes: productive uses (about two hundred parcels to grow hops, crops, orchards, and cut flowers); a greenway that stitches together a cluster of vacant lots; performative landscapes that manage stormwater; and a park in the center of the neighborhood. Such a comprehensive strategy, we feel, signaled that every vacant lot in the neighborhood has a purpose. In addition, we have crafted a catalogue of care that relates to the folks who live in the neighborhood and who have been trained to take responsibility for the ongoing maintenance of these landscapes.

The work of planning in Detroit is focused on what the landscapes can become, how we can show we value them, how to honor the stories embedded in them, and how we can raise their productive—as well as passive—qualities to a level that brings pride and practical uses to neighborhood residents. In the end, we strive to demonstrate respect for those who are there, reverence for the history of the place, appreciation of the quiet natural everyday spaces. We admit and espouse that beauty is something we all crave and should have within reach in our everyday lives. In all the work that it takes to transition the landscape into positive rather than negative urban attributes, we firmly believe that only by respecting community voices can strategies be created that truly resonate with residents' visions for the future of their city—and by such means we demonstrate that, indeed, Black landscapes do matter.

Note

Since writing this article, I accepted the offer from Chicago mayor Lori Lightfoot to be her commissioner of planning and development. From a distance, I continue to take a deep interest in Detroit and its regeneration through productive landscape strategies and community engagement. I know that I left planning in Detroit in the hands of a highly professional and dedicated team.

SITE OF THE UNSEEN

The Racial Gaming of American Landscapes

Austin Allen

As they traverse the urban landscapes of New Orleans, the Mardi Gras Indians (known also as the Black Indians of New Orleans) often reference "the game." This "game" refers to a set of thoroughly remembered and complex layering of rules, rituals, interpretations, negotiations, and African and Native American cultural confluences communicated to each other and to other Mardi Gras Indian tribes.[1]

Though one can hear the Mardi Gras Indians coming from blocks away, the routes are always held secret and sacred. The Black Indian landscape nodes or destination points are known—for instance, "under the bridge"—but the temporal movement through space is relative (for example, will the Mardi Gras Indians be there at three o'clock, or will they not appear today?). Without this uncertainty of movement through the American landscape, the Black landscape is incomplete. Ultimately, this "game" belongs to the tribes and is only marginally understood by most other people. As much as the tribe's pathways are sought after by thousands of people, their routes are unpredictable in timing and trajectory. The excitement, burst of colors, and imagery, created when the Indians appear in the urban landscape, make them, however, one of the most powerful cultural institutions defining New Orleans. The Indians ground us in spaces touched and seen—as well as those

The late Iberville Housing Project, New Orleans, Louisiana. Built in 1942 to replace part of the Storyville "red-light" district, its 821 units were first designated as "whites-only" and later housed African Americans. In 2013, this low-income public housing was demolished and replaced by the Bienville Basin Apartments development. (Photograph by Keith Calhoun, © Keith Calhoun McCormick)

imagined. The tribes are anchored in the culture and meaning of specific neighborhoods, and they project this meaning back to the broader community with an intensity that marks their presence on the streets of New Orleans long after the events of the day have ended.[2]

Although seemingly contradictory, elusiveness of place coupled with improvisation through time may be the essence of gaming in America—the site of the unseen. African Americans spend a great deal of time defining places in the urban and rural landscape. Black artists, authors, filmmakers, musicians, DJs, athletes, and comedians all identify and project places. In their respective 2017 tours on Netflix, Dave Chappelle and Katt Williams each spend the first ten minutes in a call-and-response with their audiences that focuses on place.[3] African Americans have come

AUSTIN ALLEN

to expect this emphasis from their culture bearers. Place is so critical in the African American discourse because, in spite of our central role of shaping and making these places, claiming them and holding onto them is elusive at best. The difficulty is that the American economic engine, from the beginning, and through force, moves African American populations across the landscape in a manner that continuously attempts to disconnect them from the wealth they generated by their hard work and their manipulation of land itself. African American culture resists this force by using improvisation and defining places in an attempt to claim an identity tied to real soil and pavements—to landscapes. The struggle to define place, which transpires devoid of historical realities and without those who shaped the place in order to generate capital, is the American Game.

In a recent YouTube video that has over 7.3 million hits, a British-accented voice warns foreigners traveling or relocating to the United States to avoid "12 of the Worst Places to Live in the U.S.A."[4] The voice gives a short audio synopsis set to visual imagery of postapocalyptic urbanism centered around major problems in each of those cities. The narrative focuses on the epidemics that plague the dozen locations, including overwhelming numbers of crime victims, rampant and raging gang violence, massive unemployment, a plethora of murders and other major criminal acts, the worst air and ground pollution in America, and rampant opiate drug addiction. Conspicuously not detailed is the makeup of those "unfortunate" urban locales. In each of these twelve cities, African Americans and Hispanics average 63.9 percent of the inhabitants, with median populations 43 percent African American and 20.9 percent Hispanic.

Three of those cities have been my place of residence. I have considered each of them my home, at least for a critical stay of some years in each place, starting with Oakland (ranking nine), New Orleans (number eight), and, Cleveland (number three), where the video features an abandoned building on whose second floor I once lived. If that were not enough, my father is buried on the outskirts of this list's number-one worst city, Camden, New Jersey. I like and identify with these complicated urban spaces—they are places that have helped me understand why the gaming of race is the central organizer of the American city as well as the American landscape, and why Black landscapes matter. Africans, because of their knowledge and through chattel slavery, were brought to the Americas to reshape the landscape.[5]

One would never grasp this understanding by looking at the profession of landscape architecture, in which African Americans are barely seen, though they should have a major influence.

When landscapes have been defined as "Black landscapes," the gaming of the American landscape has failed. The American landscape hides how African Americans have built so much of the foundation of the United States; instead, it reveals historical inaccuracies. Defining these places gives us a more accurate read of our country and offers a means to build a more relevant and equitable society. But, first, it is important to understand the way African Americans have moved through the land, either by choice or by outside force. Louisiana represents one of the most striking examples of the phenomenon. In order to fully grasp how gaming, history, and place come together in the American landscape, in the following pages I explore the nomadic search for Black landscapes, the problem with history, the opening of cities, and postapocalyptic urbanism in New Orleans. Finally, I conclude with a discussion of the role of education in celebrating Black landscapes.

The Nomadic Search for Black Landscapes

I often drive when I could fly. It is my nomadic search for a tactile presence in a time and place. Much of my immediate family, including my mom, now live in Atlanta (a city that is not one of the twelve). I like traveling from New Orleans to Atlanta, which was referred to, years ago, as the "Black Mecca," at once a location for regular pilgrimage and a place to be desired.[6] In modern *Green Book* fashion,[7] there are at least two main ways to drive an automobile across Louisiana, Mississippi, Alabama, and Georgia that allow one to arrive in Atlanta with some reflection along the journey instead of being overwhelmed by "driving while Black." Both routes reveal and conceal memories while providing codes of evidence that Black lives shaped these environments.

Both routes entail staying on or close to the freeway. On rare occasion have I ventured off the main roads, which prompted my former colleague Kevin Risk, who studies slavery in Mississippi, to suggest I travel a third way, along the Natchez Trace Parkway from Natchez to Jackson, Mississippi. It was a mystical, haunting, and slow ride at 3:00 a.m., not another automobile in sight for miles, rain beating down upon the historic Native American trail. Wildcat, raccoon, deer, and unidentified animal eyes stared back at my car from the side of the road and, sometimes, from the yellow dividing line in the middle. I listened to Jackson-based blues and R&B on the radio for a calming influence. Not the best way to get to Black Mecca, if you are anyways in a hurry.

One of the main ways to Atlanta continues along I-10 East across Lake Pontchartrain, skirts along the Gulf coast to Mobile, and then heads northeast on I-65. This route passes Black markers that I have deemed important to me, my family, and many others, through the memories of Black Panthers roaming in the Lowndes County landscape. It passes Montgomery, the home of the Equal Justice Initiative's recently constructed museum dedicated as a national lynching memorial, and the destination of the Selma to Montgomery marches — landscapes powerfully reimagined by film director Ava DuVernay and others in a time warp that circumnavigates prevailing contemporary bucolic narratives defining these places.[8]

Heading farther northeast on I-85, one passes Tuskegee, home of a critical hub of Black landscape rituals planted in the countryside. Beyond Robert Taylor, at least three major forces in Black landscapes and the Tuskegee experience define this land: George Washington Carver; landscape architect David Williston; and artist and landscape architect Edward L. Pryce, FASLA.

Sometimes I take a quick detour here to Union Springs and Enon, the plantation of my father's family. The plantation is about 1,400 acres, still active and accessible to the public. And, within the Black landscape of the plantation lies another Black landscape. Through the main entrance, to the center, is a cemetery where lie generations of African Americans — according to my relatives, layers of unmarked graves atop unmarked graves. Adjacent to the cemetery is an African Methodist Episcopal (AME) church that was rebuilt after it burned down in 1964. I feel enriched walking the grounds, reading the gravestones that date no later than the late 1800s, and remembering my ancestors. I then get back on I-85 toward Atlanta.

Even with all those attractions, my preferred route is through Mississippi. Crossing Lake Pontchartrain, I almost immediately turn northeast on I-59, a beautiful freeway on which one rides through the shade of pines and magnolias, past Hattiesburg, into Jones County and Laurel, and onward to Meridian. All this before arriving in Birmingham, which is number seven on the list, and so full of Black landscapes one could dwell on Sixteenth Street for an eternity and keep discovering them.

In Meridian, I frequently stop to get refueled. I like stopping in Meridian for its name and its place in memory. Meridian has many definitions: from a classical Chinese acupuncture perspective, "meridian" refers to a channel or pathway for qi, or energy, to flow through the body; from a geographical perspective, it is a circle on the earth's surface, passing through the north and south poles.

Mainly, though, I stop in Meridian to remember. Similar to the twelve cities, 62 percent of Meridian's population of forty thousand is African American.

I specifically take James Chaney Drive, Exit 151, where two gas stations sit at the edge of a small city. Strangely, as of this writing, there is no James Chaney Drive, nor any road signs or directions to anything about James Chaney upon departing the freeway. If one heads south, however, on what is called Valley Drive for about four miles, and takes a slight turn to the left, goes up the hill, and glances to the right, James Chaney's gravestone is visible from the street. If one goes north instead, into the city, Forty-Ninth Street does change into James E. Chaney Drive once it crosses over the railroad tracks.

Nothing significant stands out about Exit 151 over any other exits in this Mississippi landscape. Nevertheless, I have made this my ritual stopping. Here, brutality and repression have been neatly hidden into a landscape shaped by Black lives. In *What Is Landscape?*, John R. Stilgoe explains, "With care, inquirers can understand the landscape conjurings of others, but only rarely can they escape, even momentarily, the contemporary mindset."[9]

Tom Dent's book *Southern Journey* helped me understand the Mississippi game.[10] When I was working on the documentary *Claiming Open Spaces* (1995), Dent was finishing *Southern Journey*.[11] He understood the Mississippi landscape as an insider; on many occasions, in New Orleans, he delayed talking to me about my own research on the city until 3:00 a.m. at a sidewalk table at Café Brasil,[12] where we could look into the window to see and hear the music but could also hear each other talk. Near the end of his book, Dent hauntingly circumnavigates Meridian, tracing Chaney's steps.

At the beginning of the book, Dent quotes Frederick Law Olmsted, the founder of American landscape architecture: "I begin to suspect that the great trouble and anxiety of Southern gentlemen is, how, without quite destroying the capabilities of the negro for any work at all, to prevent him from learning to take care of himself."[13] Game recognizing game, Olmsted understood he identified only half of the problem. How to make the slaves forget to remember they built all this with their own historical knowledge of landscape was even more troublesome to contemplate.

In Meridian, I struggle to make sense of what happened in the centuries leading to 1964, and the following decades until now. In 1964, the AME church burned down on my family's plantation. It was part of an organized campaign, not only to intimidate by burning down churches but also to remove evidence of Black landscapes in America.

I suspect many others take Exit 151 to pay respect to Chaney. There is something different in the way people speak to each other, with an extra politeness, in that Pilot gas station, like we are all looking for some way to express what could have been and what might still be possible in this brief place and time. What is landscape, if not that expression? Standing on Meridian soil—rich, black soil—begs for the Kevin Lynch question, "What time is this place?"

Mrs. Mable Hoskins Oatis of the Wechsler Foundation tells me you have to go back to 1894, thirty years after the end of the Civil War.[14] It was a war about economics but, more importantly, one about Black landscapes—a war not about whether Black landscapes matter but, like El Dorado, about whether they ever even existed in the Western Hemisphere. The American Civil War was about the control and defining of landscapes: Whose were they? Who designed them? Who built them? Who benefited? Who remembered and defined these places and gave them the desired meaning in order to ensure power for future generations?

Naming Black landscapes with other names has been a survival technique that often keeps these places in safe harbor, exemplified by my paternal family's involvement in the history of Wilberforce University, in Ohio. An uncle (actually one of my father's cousins) hinted that the second-oldest historically Black college and university was not named after a famous African American but after William Wilberforce, a famously antislavery Englishman—so that it would not be targeted for demolition. Nonetheless, the university's original building was burned down the night that President Lincoln was assassinated.[15]

When I started screening *Claiming Open Spaces,* some audience members demanded to know the exact contribution of African Americans to the American landscape. Many sincerely wanted to know what had happened beyond the labor of planting, plowing, and producing for others. The research of people like Carl Anthony provided me with a list of evidentiary activities and sites throughout the South that showed that we African Americans have actively shaped the environment.[16] Those answers, however, left me unsatisfied; the structure of the question always came off as, "We Americans built one of the greatest countries ever, with great agriculture, the best modern cities, and infrastructure envied by the rest of the world, and by the way, what did your people do?" No matter how I assert otherwise, the question forces one into a defensive posture.

Brenda Marie Osbey, Louisiana's poet laureate from 2005 to 2007, gave an answer in *Claiming Open Spaces* that could be used throughout the African American existence within the built environment: "But if you look at it really closely, I think, you can see the importance of improvisational skill, the importance of being able to do it, to create a thing of beauty with exactitude and precision, there on the spot." Beauty is an ability to command recognition: I am present and compelling! Slavery by its very existence is a subterfuge, a displacement of knowledge and making in a manner that games those receiving the message—even the knowledge keeper or doer. James Chaney was in the building trade like his father, a precision-driven plasterer: a skill straight out of African origins. In spite of celebrating beauty in the American landscape, Chaney's great-grandfather was killed for not handing his land over to white people.[17]

Ultimately, what is not told in Meridian then or today pulls us back into our vehicles. We are pulled back across a complicated and contested landscape of pain brought on by what has happened and not been expressed, by a yearning to celebrate all that we know about Black contributions to the land, and in the face of centuries of a constructed denial of those factors. I leave Meridian wanting to cherish small steps toward a more accurate read of what has been created as the American landscape and the hidden Black presence upon the continent.

A family photograph shows Allen's family at the Big Walnut Country Club, one of the first African American country clubs in the United States and today the site of Friendship Park in Gahanna, Ohio, late 1920s or early 1930s. The palimpsest of pathways and building foundations—themselves codes of memories—links the existing park and a Black landscape. (Photograph courtesy of Austin Allen)

The Problem with History

That's the problem with history, we like to think it's a book—that we can turn the page and move the fuck on. But history isn't the paper it's printed on. It's memory, and memory is time, emotions, and song.
—Paul Beatty, *The Sellout*

Paul Beatty pierces through the gamed sense of place to another reality. When he begins to write about history, we begin to understand the divergence, notably in the

African American community, between history and codes of memory: the historical is often the official record of the moment, and the codes of memory are our only means for anchoring our thoughts in a world we can hold as authentic.

The photo on page 105, from my family's collection, taken in the late 1920s or early 1930s, captures an outing at the Big Walnut Country Club, founded in 1927. Today it is the site of Friendship Park in Gahanna, Ohio. More than the written history, codes of memory, like this photo, link the existing park and a Black landscape, one of the first African American country clubs founded in the United States. The popular park is frequented by all races, but I think most contemporary users have little to no knowledge of how the park came to be, or why there are steps down to the water and foundations on-site predating the park. I spent many childhood summers in and around the Black-owned cottages, or in a rowboat with cousins in the middle of Big Walnut Creek, and later in life walking the perimeter with my uncles in a homegoing ritual.

Occasionally, I think about another native of Columbus, Ohio: Rahsaan Roland Kirk. Blinded at two years old, he became an internationally celebrated jazz musician known for simultaneously playing multiple instruments and producing unique sounds that he called "Black classical music." Kirk's music was inspired by his dreams, which he believed. He often saw landscapes in them. In listening to the dialogues that precede many of his songs, I cannot help but perceive landscape and place in his words. Like his music, I sense his approach to landscape unique, improvised from dreams, marked by his sightlessness. He offers visions of a Black vernacular where the elusiveness of place can be seen or experienced if one seeks awareness of the layers surrounding them.

In 1972, he recorded a version of "The Old Rugged Cross," an old spiritual hymnal. Over the years, I have come to consider his rendition as a song about Black landscapes. It's like a "stations of the crossroad," a way of approaching the intersections of life choices that we all must face from time to time. Here, Kirk places twelve different crosses in the landscape. Perhaps they are signs to negotiate a hostile environment: the literal ones, which include the Black Cross, Green Cross, White Cross, Double Cross, Cross on Your Shoulder, and Old Rugged Cross; as well as the six inferred ones, signs of the conflicts and struggle that await us—the Lost Cross, Cross to Get Across, Crossed Up, Crossed on the Cross, Crisscross, and the Cross

We Must Bear. Typical of Kirk, his song is spiritual, but without orthodoxy: he pulls religion to a space within which he navigated, one with an African American sense.

In thinking about where those searching can experience such a complicated landscape, like this one Kirk portrays in central Ohio, I have returned to Big Walnut Creek. At least one place has stood out. It clearly contains contradictory messages. The place is hidden in plain sight—it's invisible in one sense and yet visible to those who choose to reframe the site. Years before the dams and freeways were built, one could walk or, during the right season, take a small rowboat north, up Big Walnut Creek, from what was once the Black resort in Gahanna (now Friendship Park) for ten miles. After heading west for about four miles on what is now called Big Walnut Road, one arrived at that crossroad. Nowadays, this crossroad is a nondescript intersection, with an old church for sale on one side, the massive Alum Creek dam on another.

Those who read the signs in this mostly white suburban part of the countryside will see the road name gives away its history: Africa Road. I first saw the name on a map when I was in my late teens, and I tried to make sense of it, seemingly displaced, given that no African Americans lived there. I drove searching for the road and missed it, thrown off course by a new freeway and the dam. Later I learned it was a main route of the Underground Railroad. The small church was one of the major stations on that road to the North and Canada.

Crossroads are an important part of Black landscapes because of the cultural ties that link at least four continents together—Africa, Europe, North and South America. And, like most Black landscapes in the United States, they remain hidden with only tricksters—ever-present entities across the African cultural diaspora—to give an indication of the gravity of the moment as one chooses how to navigate the landscape. One can make a decision and not even know that they are making it. One can blindly ignore the obvious for not seeing, and miss the opportunities to understand, to grow with a new level of comprehending the human condition.

The landscape architect Doug Williams champions an understanding that African American authors, especially writers of fiction, have articulated the impact of Blacks on the American landscapes, and even more than those in the planning and design disciplines. Williams's arguments often start by critiquing the writings of the late author Toni Morrison, whose stories are anchored in an examination of cultures, places, and times. Morrison interrogates the African American country clubs of a not too distant past. In *Beloved,* Morrison focuses upon a woman caught in Cincinnati, in the 1800s, at the borderline between overt slavery and a kind of freedom for African Americans that was as complicit in slavery as the trade itself.[18] In contemporary times, African Americans often experience "the urban" United States, yet African Americans do not have many opportunities to participate in officially defining, planning, or designing where the trash bin is located, let alone the house, apartment, street, neighborhood, infrastructure, or central business district.

African Americans do, however, imagine, and within fiction lies the greater reality of the contestation of urban space presently and in historical terms. From fiction comes not so fictional narratives, like the works of Octavia Butler.[19] Gloria Naylor's *The Women of Brewster Place* explains a place and time within Baltimore, and Tayari Jones examines a contemporary Atlanta and Louisiana in her 2018 novel, *An American Marriage.*[20] The Compton of our recent memory becomes Beatty's neighborhood of Dickens. Teju Cole's *Open City* is New York City: "It never ceases to surprise me how easy it is to leave the hybridity of the city and enter into all-white spaces, the homogeneity of which, as far as I can tell, causes no discomfort to the whites in them."[21]

John Edgar Wideman's Homewood within Pittsburgh is the subject in the novel *Fanon.* Wideman's persona takes the filmmaker Jean Luc Godard to Homewood to explain the history of this urban space: "Let me be clear from the outset. We didn't do this neighborhood to ourselves. Neither we negroes who inhabit the dead end where we're stuck nor we Americans doomed to undertake the task of saving a world we fear by destroying it first."[22]

The statement begs the question, "Who did do it then?" Chester Himes's investigations hint at the answer in *If He Hollers Let Him Go* (1945), a novel about a quickly evolving Los Angeles. Of housing, the character Arline says: "And you know how they'll do even if they build a development down there; they will allocate about one-fourth to Negroes and the rest to whites and Mexicans."[23]

A host of noir novel writers, including Walter Mosley, went further in depth about "the who," in Los Angeles. In the years before 1964, the rapid and sustained mass movements of African Americans from the rural to the urban included the movement of African Americans to Los Angeles from the South, both disrupting and initiating a racial dislocation of place. In *The Warmth of Other Suns,* Isabel Wilkerson documents the evacuation of six million African Americans from the rural South to the urban North and West of the United States, starting in World War I and continuing through the 1970s. She writes, "As he settled in for the twenty-three-hour train ride up the coast of the Atlantic, he had no desire to have anything to do with the town he grew up in, the state of Florida, or the South as a whole, for that matter."[24] Bridgett M. Davis gives a sense of what waited in the North in her 2019 memoir, *The World According to Fannie Davis: My Mother's Life in the Detroit Numbers.*

The difficulty of defining and assigning value to Black landscapes is in the disassociation. In this difficulty lies the struggle of African Americans to press ahead with increasing codes of memory necessitated by the dislocation of southern African Americans from a firm association with specific land and landscapes. History must be communicated with the full recognition of its fictions and a greater clarity must be provided by the people who sacrificed and made the codes of memory. For instance, the city of New Orleans, built and imagined mainly by enslaved African Americans, free and enslaved Haitians, and hosts of other oppressed people, celebrated its three-hundredth anniversary in 2018. How and who will tell the story of that place in future decades?

In New Orleans, the removal of Confederate statues as a means to alter and recognize the gaming aspects of urbanism has moved across the South. The defeat of the Confederate States of America by the Union army, in 1865, was only a first step toward defeating racism as the central organizer of American landscapes. Confederate sculptures were built long after the end of the Civil War to reinforce the enslavement or subservience of African Americans to a system far after its supposed ending. They were built less to commemorate and more to keep the narratives of these lands obfuscated in myth and denial and to enforce an ordered hierarchy. For instance, "Congo Square" in New Orleans, one of the most significant Black landscapes in America, and recognized as such by local and international populations, was purposefully and officially misnamed as "P. G. T. Beauregard Square," after a Confederate general, from 1893 until 2011.[25]

Race effectively structured the United States so that the economic gain of a few could be justified by the premise that they were white and born with the innate potential to become wealthy. This premise was reinforced by the ability to define and name in celebration one's superiority over nonwhites, as the Confederate sculptures did.

The distortion had become so askew by the Civil War that millions of whites could still believe, over decades following the war, that it was acceptable and nonconsequential to live in a democracy or a republic where facades, parades, and a cultural way of life advocated for a continuation of the massacre and enslavement of one set of human beings over another. Worse, this disassociation from reality, tied to the erasure of the African American presence within the landscape, continues to keep most Americans living in a video game–like perception of place, where interchangeable, imaginary, and fantasy-laced landscapes set a backdrop for a skewed idea of what is or could ever be thought of as authentic.

Early on, even before the Civil War had started, ex-slaves and many white Americans, including the founding father of American landscape architecture, Olmsted, whether conscious of this or not, saw that education tied to landscape was an effective and critical tool for countering the oppressive, violent psychological and physical enslavement of African Americans. Education as enlightenment could make others see and identify an African existence: Black landscapes as not only feasible but essential in the shaping of the Western Hemisphere. Olmsted proposed the Port Royal experiment in South Carolina, where ex-slaves would receive education on an island they had designed and built, and develop a recognition of their own worth and identity before their integration into the republic.[26] One of the great believers in education was Saint Katharine Drexel and the Sisters of the Blessed Sacrament, who saw the construction of African American and Native American Catholic schools as the means of eliminating discrimination and dire poverty among their communities.[27] Saint Katharine's schools enabled African Americans to anchor cultural roots to the land and to a place, and provided a structured approach to making sustainable, racially identified institutions across America. Saint Katharine donated the initial funds for the building of Saint Joseph Church and School, in Meridian, and, by 1915, she had done the same for Xavier University, in New Orleans.[28] The list of alumni from both institutions speaks to the tremendous impact of her contributions in creating Black landscapes where survival was based upon improvisation, there on the spot.

The Opening of Cities

Cole's *Open City* had no arbitrary title; nor did Lee Sang-Ki's 2008 film *Open City* (2008); nor Roberto Rossellini's *Rome, Open City* (1945); Ipek Türeli's *Istanbul, Open City: Exhibiting Anxieties of Urban Modernity* (2018); Eddie Romero's *Manila, Open City* (1968); Samir Habchi's *Beirut Open City* (2008); nor Mitra Mansouri's documentary *Bam, Open City* (2005).[29] Nor were the titles of dozens of other narratives of the same name arbitrary. They sought to examine the complexity and pitfalls of creating negotiated urban environments. Hundreds of narratives under less obvious titles, such as Colson Whitehead's *Zone One* (2012), Carol Reed's *The Third Man* (1949), and even Issa Rae's *Insecure* or Phoebe Waller-Bridge's *Fleabag* do similarly, often within a threatening or volatile setting.[30] All have attempted to clarify the importance of urban cultural landscapes in improving the human condition. They peel back layers to keep a level of negotiated civility in the process to outweigh the indirect threat, or direct acts, of violence associated with defining cities. Cole examines these layers and histories of New York City: "The site was a palimpsest, as was all of the City, written, erased, rewritten. There had been communities here before Columbus ever set sail. Before Verrazano anchored his ships in the narrows or the black Portuguese slave trader Esteban Gómez sailed up the Hudson; human beings had lived here, built homes, and quarreled with their neighbors long before the Dutch ever saw a business opportunity. . . . Generations rushed through the eye of the needle, and I, one of the still legible crowd, entered the subway."[31]

There are facts, myths, and there are truths about cities, their landscapes, their canons, and of course, their cannons. Take, for instance, Baton Rouge and New Orleans. Both cities sit along the Mississippi River and benefited, in growth, from plantation life. At first glance, they have much alike, and a similar promise. Baton Rouge is the center of politics, the state capital of Louisiana, and holds a legacy of southern traditions. New Orleans is larger, and its active port has established its position as both an economic and cultural hub—within the Caribbean, and globally. Both cities have a majority population of African Americans in a state that has a 34 percent African American population.

Both, also, have experienced recent endeavors for secession. The wealthier, white portion of Baton Rouge in the southern portion of East Baton Rouge Parish attempted, in an effort to resegregate educational institutions, to form a separate city called Saint George. The secession failed initially, but the bitter divide remained between the southern and northern portions of the parish.[32] On October 12, 2019, voters approved the creation of Saint George but have yet to legally sanction it; a lawsuit countering the secession includes residents in the area and Baton Rouge mayor Sharon Weston Broome. In 2017, prior to the tenures of the current mayor and Council member, a movement started in the African American and Vietnamese areas of New Orleans East (the East) to consider secession from New Orleans.[33] The East believed the city was becoming an apartheid landscape where economic development and wealth happened mainly in the older part of New Orleans, while the East was perpetually delivered unrealized promises for a better quality of life. The election of both the mayor and councilperson for the East arose in part as a response to this alienation. As, however, the gap widens in the urban American experience between the rich and poor, and between the landscapes with services and without services, threats of secession will likely increase in multiple urban centers.

The difference between the secession movements of these cities reflects two canons of thought that describe where African Americans are positioned in the urban landscape. One views African Americans as participants in the growth of society; the other sees them as the root of most of its problems. Historically, New Orleans was the northernmost Caribbean city culturally oriented as a major slave-trading hub serving as an interface between Caribbean landscapes and southern landscapes near or adjacent to the Mississippi River. Baton Rouge was a major stop going downriver, a southern city known for multiple institutions, burdened with the gaming of divisions and strengthened by a mentality that held subjugation and enslavement as normative behaviors. Both cities claim legacies of slavery, and a violent aftermath that continues the conditioning of that institution upon the land. Both must move rapidly to reconcile this dilemma with their own populations, with the populations who travel to these destinations, and with the collective will to be identified in modern terms as an "open city." Both are driven by negotiations that are, at least, based upon ideas of a just behavior in contemporary Louisiana.

If one travels to the flagship Louisiana State University (LSU) in Baton Rouge for a football game, one will see two cannons in front of the LSU ROTC Building.

These two cannons fired the first shots at Fort Sumter, South Carolina, starting the Civil War. General William Tecumseh Sherman, the first superintendent of LSU before the war, gave the cannons to LSU as a gift indicating the war's end. There can be reconciliation, there can be healing, his gift attempted to say. The gift was about finding a way back to the possibility of America.

Sherman is considered one of the first generals of modern warfare, burning Meridian to the ground in 1864, one hundred years before Chaney's death, and burning Atlanta to the ground later that same year.[34] His actions likely contributed to the initial use of the term "open city," a war term that meant that the cultural value of a certain city was worth preserving and outweighed the military benefit of its total destruction.[35] In Western civilization, the declaration of an open city gave opposing armies the opportunity to negotiate the preservation of a place. It inextricably linked the urban to a cautious downscaling of violent actions in the hope of an agreed-upon peace within the internal borders of a city.

In early 1865, Sherman recognized the abilities and legacies of African Americans in shaping landscapes: he bequeathed each postenslavement family "forty acres and a mule."[36] While many see this as a compensation for slavery, Sherman understood that these forty acres included thirty miles inland along the coastline, the part of the United States that physically most resembled West Africa. Africans and their descendants would have no problem working this land because they had obviously worked it for the past couple hundred years to the benefit of the whole nation. Congress also understood the land's resemblance, and the implications this had for land ownership in the United States. They rescinded the gift immediately after the end of the war.[37] LSU, on the other hand, maintained its gifts, leaving out the part about the slaves, and remained a segregated institution for another one hundred years, until the class of 1964.

In America after the Civil War, like at LSU, race and racism as an institution strengthened as the central organizer of the American city. American urbanism was subjected to the suppression of reason and truths, the further obfuscation of place by massive redlining, redistricting, eventual urban renewal, and the cyclical removal of entire neighborhoods to clean the slate (yet again) in order to destabilize the city and redline it (once more) in a never-ending real estate gaming process. The collective examination of race, housing, and the American city lays bare urban conflict at its heart. Embattled but tenacious individuals like Jane Jacobs and Frank Horne understood activism, sacrifice, and struggle as the necessary tools to counter the massive impact of race and class upon housing and social policies, as witnessed in the housing booms and tragic failures over the past seven decades. Of Jacobs, Roberta Brandes Gratz said, "She found in the city a dynamic energy, a vitality from the absence of control, the ability of so many positive things made possible exactly because of people's ability to self-organize for civic, economic, or social purposes."[38] Richard Sennett added further praise: "The idea of an open city is not my own: credit for it belongs to the great urbanist Jane Jacobs in the course of arguing against the urban vision of Le Corbusier. . . . She believes that in an open city, as in the natural world, social and visual forms mutate through chance variation; people can best absorb, participate, and adapt to change if it happens step by lived step. This is evolutionary urban time, the slow time needed for an urban culture to take root."[39] Going even further, Jacobs writes, "Sometimes, to be sure, a deliberate conspiracy to turn over the population of a neighborhood does exist—on the part of real estate operators who make a racket of buying houses cheaply from panicked white people and selling them at exorbitant prices to the chronically housing-starved and pushed-around colored population."[40]

Horne, a noted Harlem Renaissance poet, optometrist, college president, and celebrated housing expert, explained the meaning of the open city and its relationship to urban dwellers: "During times of war, it is not uncommon for a large metropolis to be declared an 'open city' to spare its residents the ravages of armed conflict. I would like to consider here another kind of conflict and another kind of open city . . . built upon three solid foundations: 1) Revised concept of neighborhoods 2) Destruction of every vestige of the separate-but-equal concept 3) Substitution of heterogeneity for homogeneity."[41]

Horne, like many contemporary writers, saw the open city as a future site of possibilities for a more just and open society.[42] The postwar period of 1945 through the late 1950s was foundational to the "racial dislocation of place" becoming a central organizing tool of both the public and private American housing industry. During that time, Horne used the legal and moral tools of integration to attempt, from inside government, to slow or halt this exploitive and antidemocratic process. Simultaneously, he used the transformative definition of an open city to touch the imagination of those on the outside of government, and as a means of articulating what form a postracial, equitable urban America might take.

In 1954, Horne envisioned the proliferation of open cities across the United States after the Supreme Court ruling *Brown v. Board of Education of Topeka* (1954), which reversed *Plessy v. Ferguson* (1896).[43] One year later, in 1955, the Eisenhower administration fired Horne, ending what historian Arnold R. Hirsch called "his seventeen-year tenure as the most outspoken, high-ranking minority official in the nation's housing agencies."[44] Horne clearly understood that the public housing projects specifically accommodating African Americans and people of color were, with deliberate speed, turning from the beacon of hope and mobility of 1937 into segregated warehouses devoid of any relationship between the tenets and the design, construction, or landscapes of place. In 1956, as the executive director of the New York Commission on Intergroup Relations, Horne delivered a speech to the Women's City Club of New York, stating:

> The very fact that New York's public housing program has been so uniquely pointed up in the national scene as a successful example of sound integration makes all the more alarming the apparent reversals suffered during the past few years . . . Danger signal number one is the steady increase in the proportion of occupancy by non-white minority and ethnic groups in public housing. Program-wise, this proportion has now crossed the fifty-percent mark. Project-wise, there are over 30 developments in which occupancy by Negro, Puerto Rican, and Chinese tenants is in excess of sixty-percent of the total occupancy. Of these, ten are so preponderantly occupied by non-white minorities that we cannot escape identifying them as veritable racial ghettos.[45]

These spaces, the projects, were also simultaneously starting to be defined erroneously as Black landscapes by the dominant society, particularly as resources became scarcer for maintaining them. African Americans improvised in these spaces, but they were not the designers or the owners. Horne answered clearly the Wideman question of, "Who did it then?"

A new understanding of the open city was emerging, and it was useful for imagining the possibilities of a diverse, sustainable, and democratic city. This version was rooted in the 1945 publication of Karl R. Popper's *The Open Society and Its Enemies*.[46] Popper offered a forward-looking philosophy to a Western world reeling from a decade of world-war devastation, where cities exemplified one of the most visible symbols of that devastation, but also the hope for the future.

Popper's ideas gained expression both in the Open Housing movement and within the concept of integration, as part of the civil rights movement. Because of integration, the resulting massive "racial dislocation of place" further obscured insight into Black landscapes. Race became ahistorical when tied to the individual pursuit of integrating public and private housing in America devoid of a substantial connection to landscape. In 1967, Harold Cruse, in his seminal work *The Crisis of the Negro Intellectual,* criticizes the "open society" because it placed ideas of the individual over collective movement and knowledge in this regard: "Thus the Negro integrationist runs afoul of reality in the pursuit of an illusion, the 'open society'—a false front that hides several doors to several different worlds of hyphenated-Americans. Which group or subgroup leaves its door wide open for the outsider? None really."[47]

Cruse spent a great deal of time dissecting an integrationist approach to the open society, and thus also the open city itself, because of its inability to deal with the cultural identity of place. In his case, a cultural Harlem juxtaposed with the elimination of African American space in Hansberry's *A Raisin in the Sun* exemplifies that preclusive cultural identity. He also examined the book's tie to the *Hansberry v. Lee* U.S. Supreme Court case decided on November 12, 1940, on race, housing, and the right to move out of a particular history:

> As long as the Negro's cultural identity is in question, or open to self-doubts, then there can be no positive identification. . . . [W]ithout a cultural identity that adequately defines himself, the Negro cannot even identify with the American nation as a whole . . . alienated and directionless on the landscape of America, in a variegated nation of Whites who have not yet decided on their own identity. . . . It is the Negro movement's impact that . . . forces the whole nation to look into itself—which it has never wanted to do.[48]

The other kind of open city in design and planning disciplines and professions has come to be known as a place where movements of growth, equity, justice, and

AUSTIN ALLEN

vision parallel developments in interpersonal relationships. In an interview, Kees Christiaanse stated, "'Open city' is a somewhat utopian term: it refers to efforts by architects and urban designers to translate the ideals of an 'open society'—a society with a tolerant and inclusive government, where diverse groups develop flexible mechanisms for resolving inevitable differences—into physical spaces."[49]

While open cities may provide a way to create a discourse for equity, they often fail to recognize the cultural identity of place. Moreover, they cannot offer equity without recognizing that Black landscapes exist, that they define a people, and thus define America. Like Jacobs, Cruse sought to define place—Harlem—in relationship to time as a means of strengthening that identity and that argument. And thus, the pursuit of openness becomes both a dream and a nightmare about the origins and the future of the urban landscape, caught between a recognition of what has happened and what might go wrong without reconciling with the past.

Open cities and catastrophic events often exist in tandem. They may even be intertwined in a way that can advance both the power of culture and the possibilities within a built environment. As abstract as that may seem, the mass destruction of built environments gave rise to the words "open city." The brutal contrast of the immediate removal of a place that may have taken centuries to evolve—into a central nerve for commerce, education, spiritual reflection, and sustaining life—is at best numbing to the soul. Hence, the devastation of entire cities during the Civil War necessitated the creation of a modern response to avoid complete annihilation of a cultured civilization. It also perversely allowed for the cleansing of history through a hierarchical preservation of places while erasing and rewriting the importance of other landscapes. This manner of erasure has caused this nation to darken its view upon, and even doubt, its own early structural frameworks of how landscapes and economies were formed.

Postapocalyptic Urbanism

Like a wiped-out history or memory, postapocalyptic stories exist without a full context. I grew up immersed in postapocalyptic stories, behind whose narratives was the ever-present question, "Who did the apocalypse, and why?"

It was starting to get dark on the evening of November 7, 2005. I was in New Orleans, driving up Poland Road to France Street, leaving the Lower Ninth Ward and heading to New Orleans East. At the top of the bridge where France Street becomes Alvar Street, I could see, on my left, the ruins of the new housing in the Desire Development Neighborhood. No one else was in sight. I flashed back, decades, to my childhood, sitting in the backseat of a car. My parents were watching the screen at a drive-in movie, on which Harry Belafonte, in a tuxedo, walked through the streets of New York without another soul around. The movie showing was *The World, the Flesh and the Devil,* a 1959 narrative that inextricably links the postapocalyptic to race.[50]

My former colleague Joseph Juhasz, referring to *The Third Man* (1949), explained that there is always a spiritual and temporal tension between the apocalyptic event and the postapocalyptic: World War II was the apocalyptic; the life in Vienna after the war the postapocalyptic. In the film, a revealing landscape of people goes about life in postwar Vienna. At the top of a Ferris wheel, the Orson Welles character, Harry, says to the Joseph Cotton character: "Look down there. Would you really feel any pity if one of those dots stopped moving forever? If I offered you 20,000 pounds for every dot that stopped, would you really, old man, tell me to keep my money? Or would you calculate how many dots you could afford to spend?" The indeterminate point of where one moment ends and the other, the "post," begins drives the narrative's momentum. Was the apocalypse slavery, or did the apocalyptic continue as the ability to game everyone into believing that the economy and landscape built upon slave labor was simply historical, or maybe did not even happen? Was Hurricane Katrina and the consequential flooding the apocalyptic event, or part of the postapocalyptic wake, one event in a long line of abuses and destruction?

Writers, reporters, and critics commonly opt for the term "dystopia," but the word is much too tranquil against a postapocalyptic landscape where one slips easily back and forth between apocalyptic and postapocalyptic. African American life has often slid between these bookends: from the arbitrary lynching of some as a means of slowing the economic and social gain of the many; to the complete destruction of towns or parts of cities to expedite the removal of people, thus halting or reversing a community's successful economic or social growth.

AUSTIN ALLEN

I have thought about this annihilation while traveling on I-10 through Baton Rouge to Lafayette, up I-49 to Shreveport, Louisiana, along I-20, then into Texas. During recent trips I have reflected on Ron Chernow's book *Grant* (2017), specifically, his accounts of post–Civil War events.[51] Grant managed a peculiar balancing act: he enforced peace as whites reacted violently to Blacks articulating a Black landscape—a landscape that reflected hundreds of years of working and knowing the Louisiana land. Thousands upon thousands of African Americans lost their lives post-1865 as communities and whole populations were altered or removed in cities including Colfax, Opelousas, Alexandria, Natchitoches, Shreveport, and New Orleans.

But through these deaths has come resistance. I see this resistance today when I attend funerals. I have gone to a few where the orange suit in the front row leaps out into my vision. The orange stands out as it is meant to, if not by choice of the wearer, then by the insistence of a greater power placing it against the usual black or dark wear of American funerals. At one funeral, months ago, in Baton Rouge, amid at least three hundred other people, there it was, as pronounced as ever—one orange suit in a sea of black. One young African American probably in his late twenties, shackles around his ankles, double handcuffed on the wrists, and chains connecting the two sets. A slightly older Black man in a black suit sat next to him with an arm around the prisoner's shoulder. They were in the family row. I contemplated: guard/prisoner, counselor/prisoner, mentor/mentee, or even father/son? He turned out to be the prisoner's older brother. The arm was a shelter and a connection all at once—part of a ritual around death and the celebration of homegoing. In the losing of life there is a reclaiming, even if it is ever so temporary.

It is the reclaiming of someone from a captured class that has its own imprint upon the landscape at places like Angola Prison—named after the many Angolans who once occupied the same land as slaves shaping the same landscape. Millions are part of this class nationally. It is Louisiana that has the most prisoners per capita in America.

The man in the orange suit, at different points during the service, sat pensively as people went forward to meet the family. Some hugged him, while others rendered him invisible at first—a kind of unconscious decision to not see what is too painful to witness—and then recognized the future. It was easier to leave the future confined to some other folks' reality—a future that would unfold in a bad place for, in worst cases, often no less than ten to forty years.

The suit symbolizes the building of wealth in communities surrounding the prisons, and the inextricable binding whereby one landscape is obligated to another. That funeral day, the young man paid attention to all the speakers who spoke of his mother, telling stories about almost being captured or caught up in a system. One woman, a doctor, spoke of seeing the young man's mother as a sort of modern-day Harriett Tubman, delivering so many young people to freedom. She offered them education, and advocated for utilization of the land, which, she said, could move youth and ex-prisoners closer to understanding that slavery only works when slaves accept that status.

As I drove away from the service, I thought about her son clad in the orange suit as part of a postapocalyptic landscape comprised of a beautiful green countryside and a supposedly abandoned institution. The nation has not totally freed itself from slavery's clutches.

At its core, Baton Rouge easily exhibits a problematic relationship to Black landscapes. The northern part of East Baton Rouge Parish is 77 percent African American, creating a distinct Black belt. People have lived for many generations in the northern part of East Baton Rouge. This part of the city has long been distinct from the rest of the city; the southern part of that parish has a significant white population whose wealth has historically dictated what happened in Baton Rouge. In August 2016, the Amite and Comite Rivers flooded with devastating results; many of the communities built in their watersheds and floodplains. Both Black and white people suffered because where they had settled or been placed was often adversely based upon race.

I have been conducting research around the city of Baker, with graduate students and in collaboration with Southern University. Baker is north of Baton Rouge and adjacent to East Baton Rouge Parish.[52] We have addressed the possibility of naturalizing the two-mile-long Baker Canal as part of the Comite River Diversion Project—a project that might have prevented 25 percent of the 2016 flooding, according to the U.S. Army Corps of Engineers.[53] A 1939 map reveals a beautiful part of the nearby Mississippi River, the bluff. Southern University, a historically Black land-grant university, is located here. The map shows oil refineries dumping waste directly into the swamp farther north. In 1939, the point on the river across from the swamp was called "Free Nigger Point." By 1963, it had changed to "Free Negro Point." I believe it is called Wilkerson Point today, but its code of memory means it was a significant Black landscape early on, leading to the creation of the Southern University Campus. Simultaneously, refineries and petrochemical plants grew in relation to African American life. This example demonstrates the argument by environmental justice advocates: if one wants to find a historical road map to many distinct Black landscapes, search for the industrial dumping grounds or the pollutants in the open air.

New Orleans is not simply the "Big Easy." In 2005, a big problem arose, symbolized by green dots: neighborhoods were seen as the problem, and the solution lay in how many green dots could be spent. The physical problem began with the Mississippi River Gulf Outlet (MRGO).[54] The MRGO was a fast way to move products in and out of the Port of New Orleans, and onward to Lake Pontchartrain, problematically moving salt water as well. The salt water killed the cypress trees in the protective barriers around New Orleans. Ironically, these cypress forests were also the homes of many Maroon colonies during slavery, wiped from memory by progress. When the surge from Hurricane Katrina broke the levee walls, the tidal wave impact, predominantly on the east side, broke the walls and caused massive flooding in 80 percent of the city, costing close to two thousand deaths.

I have spent time since 2005 in the Lower Ninth Ward. Many outside people felt that the damage caused by the flooding would be tidied and all matters wrapped up quickly. Flooding in this manner, however, had never happened before—not with that magnitude. Between 2005 and 2008, I saw impossible solutions offered, difficult positions taken, and a lack of transparency around process. I concluded that we in the disciplines of planning and design had not been ready. As much as we wanted to be ready, we were not ready for the level of tragedy that happened and that continues to play out today as climate change ravages vulnerable landscapes. The flooding and hurricane damage in Houston, Florida, and Puerto Rico in 2017; and again in Florida and the Carolinas in 2018; and in the Bahamas and Beaumont, Texas, in 2019, have strengthened this understanding.

Why in this decade are we still trying to decide if Black landscapes matter?

Mainly because we have gamed ourselves out of understanding what the American landscape is, whether urban or rural. The lack of openness in our cities and lack of accurateness in our histories have not helped us to understand the nomadic life placed upon African Americans. The consequent disconnect to the historical references of place dismisses a whole set of solutions for living in a disrupted ecosystem and leaves African Americans with a vulnerability to urban living. A thorough historical accounting of place reveals how out of sync the United States has become from understanding the cultural relevance of Black landscapes—or any landscape.

In a recent article in the *Chronicle for Higher Education,* historian Rashauna Johnson says of slavery in New Orleans: "I still marvel at this disconnect between how central it is—and how absent it is from the present landscape. It speaks to the volume of work necessary to completely erase the history of something that was once common knowledge."[55] It's common knowledge that New Orleans is a Black landscape. Americans must head toward a much more open conversation about the essential need to recognize African American contributions to landscape. If we do not, we will cease to converse about landscape—and retreat into a postapocalyptic nightmare.

Conclusion

The Mississippi River is the western border of Southern University. Northeast of Southern University's Agricultural Research Center is the land of Leland College, one of the first African American colleges in Louisiana, founded in 1870. Education has always played an important role in the survival of African Americans and the celebration of Black landscapes. In 2020, it may be one of the more viable ways to regenerate a meaningful interest in using Black landscapes to improve economic and cultural conditions for creating a more open and equitable country.

In higher education, a twenty-year span from 1960 to 1980 (known as the third period of higher education) was remarkable for its democratic growth sparked by the early thinking of educator Clark Kerr.[56] For instance, in the spirit of open cities, the public institutions of that time established forums where African Americans participated physically, intellectually, and culturally in the contested space of community colleges. The forums were a critical part of higher education. Yet, less than fifteen years later, the precepts that characterized this period—one of education's most celebrated and influential—had ceased to exist.

Community college systems became the fertile ground of free inquiry and enabled the articulation of powerful goals and opportunities for the poor, oppressed, disadvantaged, and alienated.[57] The communities and the community college systems did not always align in principle or practice, but the relationship was always strong and interlinked because those colleges were meant to be extensions of the surrounding neighborhoods—the problematic neighborhoods full of youth lacking access to higher education. And, the communities embraced these academic institutions with a sense of ownership.

Not so ironically, in 1967, the inaugural year of the California Community Colleges System, Clark Kerr was fired as president of its University of California (UC) system in one of the first acts by California's new governor, Ronald Reagan. Kerr was "blacklisted" by J. Edgar Hoover and the FBI.[58] What had Kerr unleashed?[59]

Kerr was the chief architect of the three-tiered California Master Plan for Higher Education of 1960, known as the California system. Its three tiers included the UC system, the California State University system, and the California Community Colleges System (CCCS). The latter was its most democratic arm and sought to educate those who could not afford higher education or who might benefit most from a two-year supportive transition before starting a profession or moving to another university system.[60] Thus, colleges were designed specifically to foster cultural diversity, greater access to higher learning institutions, and, as a consequence, a broader, ever-diversifying basis for inquiry. Whether Kerr intended to ignite communities or merely enlighten them, these institutions, by benefit of the California system, became fertile ground for applying ideas in communities, revealing African American life, and retooling approaches to problem solving in surrounding neighborhoods like never before.[61]

Because of its promise to democratize higher education, Kerr's California system became, from its start, one of the most copied models for higher education systems, nationally and internationally. Some places still use it today as a model. This new way of educating and providing access to learning, debate, and research changed the way that higher education functioned and was perceived in the coming decades, encouraging an open forum in every sense of the term.

Kerr referred to the years between 1960 and 1980 as "The Great Transformation in Higher Education." The academe changed from around 50 percent to 80 percent public, and the population grew from 3.5 to 12 million students. The open forums led to heightened awareness of the contradictory stated goals of the three-tier system, and the inequities and flaws created by initiating criteria that justified the upper two tiers. This recognition was most noted in the confrontations and unrest that occurred, in 1964, at UC Berkeley (part of the UC tier) as part of the Free Speech Movement. The 1967 and 1968 protests at San Francisco State University (within the State University tier) led to the creation of ethnic studies programs across the nation.[62] It was, however, the tier of the CCCS, as the free institutions, that assumed an even more intense, different but no less important, dimension within the new educational public discourse.

If Kerr was driven to find a way to make higher education the most accessible in the history of the universities and colleges, the bottom two tiers certainly opened up academe across racial barriers that had been in place for centuries. Though many scholars have written about Kerr's contribution to academe as a whole, they have less frequently articulated his system as a catalyst, or even essential, to a reconfiguration of Black intellectual growth tied to direct action.

Although the first community college opened in 1901, 2017 marked the fiftieth anniversary of the founding of the community college system, the direct outgrowth of the 1960 legislation philosophically that changed extensions of high school and junior colleges to a profusion of community-based institutions.[63] But before community colleges even established a foothold, they came under attack and are now fighting a serious decline. San Francisco Community College lost its accreditation in 2014 (though it did regain it). In recent years, community colleges have seen an overall downward trend in total enrollment figures. Rising tuition costs have been one of the major factors of decreasing enrollment. The previously held idea of education as a major solution to social inequities has also lost ground. Yet, these institutions are still seen as vital to many African Americans, particularly African American women.

To this day, these colleges are the institutions of higher education most accessible to the American public. For this reason, and to increase jobs and develop a greater workforce, President Obama launched America's Promise Act of 2015 that advocated free tuition for all community colleges. This was seen as a vital move to reverse the falling enrollment and waning mission.

Today, in what I call the "fourth period" of higher education, the idea of public and public access is being challenged or rapidly discarded, both at first-tier research institutions and local community colleges.[64] One of the greatest expressions of higher education in the 1960s was the open forum to transfer ideas and knowledge to a wide segment of disenfranchised Americans.

For only a short window of time, the community colleges functioned uniquely as catalyst for intellectual growth and the expansion of what I call the "open disciplines." An open discipline manifests the characteristics of traditional discipline building but also functions as the method for deconstructing other disciplines. Examples can be seen in the expansion of communications, ecology, and environmental justice disciplines in ways that lead to intersectionality. The dual nature of open disciplines as both defining and revealing has led the formalized education system to devalue them in the past. However, in this fourth period where transdisciplinary or integrative approaches to research and learning have become commonplace, or even essential, components of the academic environment, the potential for leadership from open disciplines is greater than ever. To understand this more, I will reflect upon the second period of higher education, between 1870 and 1910.[65]

Kerr talks about this period as the time when science and the German model of education and faculty governance were strengthened. But, equally important, he also saw this as the period when service or utility became a major focus for the land-grant institutions, intended to grow an industrial workforce and develop a meaningful relationship with the public (extension centers, etc.) in order to grow the nation and the democracy.

The duality reflects the further seeing and not seeing of African Americans and their influence upon the institutions and land in America. Land-grant institutions were a direct result of the Civil War. The fight to end slavery and the fight over the future of the African American population created land-grant institutions that served as catalysts for historically Black colleges and universities (HBCUs), and the broadening of the pool of who, Black and white, would or would not be educated in America. The fight to change the American political and social landscape by eradicating slavery created the public forum within American education. We, as African Americans, were thus central to the creation of land-grant institutions and their influences upon the American landscape. The African American presence is at once revealed as changing education for all, and immediately hidden again by confining African Americans to HBCUs for their own education.

J. B. Jackson opened my eyes to these acts of revealing and hiding. He explained that African slaves were brought to the Americas as labor, but they most importantly brought and represented a transfer of knowledge about agriculture, including the growing of rice, cotton, indigo, sugar, and a host of other plants in the Western Hemisphere, largely unknown by Europeans. Rather than acknowledge this contribution, it was essential to hide this transfer of knowledge in order to build an institution of slavery that would render Africans as uneducable. Thomas Jefferson's life at Monticello is likely a great reflection of this gaming model, where, spanning decades, he supposedly "singularly" identified the look, explained the culture, and named countless plants, many of them from Africa.

Although the second period of higher education was influenced by the ending of slavery, African Americans did not mutually enter the surrounding conversation until the third period. In the decades following the Civil War, although there was a consequential rethinking of economics and industry, and a further engagement and expansion of education, much was attempted to diminish the role, importance, and influence of African Americans upon almost the whole academic enterprise. By 1960, with growing anticolonialism and the civil rights movement, I believe that Kerr and others saw America and higher education at another crossroads. They identified the need for a system that would bring African American expressions into the tent in spite of societal attempts to act as if it were nonexistent. Lorraine Hansberry would write about an experience ten years earlier: "I shall never forget when Frank Lloyd Wright came and spoke at the University. . . . Later, addressing the packed hall, he attacked almost everything—and foremost among them, the building he was standing in for its violation of the organic principles of architecture. . . . I left the University shortly after to pursue an education of another kind."[66] Two years later, Ralph Ellison, who had also walked away from college, would deliver

Invisible Man, which critiqued Black landscapes intersecting with higher education.[67] With Kerr's efforts, African Americans helped to reformulate the entire arrangement of higher education, demanding definition of the democratic experience and revealing our impact to all. In the initial years after 1960, community colleges reflected and grew the vernacular of their communities.

But, as Simon Marginson makes clear in *The Dream Is Over,* the gains made in diversifying and expanding participation in the early years, led by the community college component of the California Master Plan of 1960, were eventually lost. These losses precipitated the collapse of the dream's central component: "By 2011 the Plan was 'dead or nearly so' in relation to six areas. . . . [T]he most significant was the failure . . . to sustain the central promise of 1960: the provision of access to higher education for all high school graduates who could benefit from it."[68] With the dying out of participants, it was no longer known that these institutions were built and based specifically upon place and the people within those communities.

In order to reignite the community college system, and to understand the African American impact on higher education, we need new collaborations. Community college districts must examine and strengthen relationships with grassroots community empowerment programs and strategies. Teaching, research, and service will take on developmental roles within this system to reinvigorate the way education is perceived in relation to change, and to create just and healthy urban environments. It is not enough to make these institutions free of tuition cost. It is not enough to have students pursue ways out of poverty as educated individuals chasing individual goals. Altering the intent of the colleges toward the collective survival and resilience of communities will make the difference. So, too, will institutions designed to serve those who most greatly need access to the technology, innovations, and knowledge based in higher education research, and the application of empowerment strategies from the ground up. These institutions must be tied to landscapes where people dwell. They must be as nomadic or stationary as the people served.

This collaboration can be nurtured between students, staff, and faculty to renew the community college mission: building resilience, responsible entrepreneurship and commerce, democratic governance, real diversity, and sustainable environmental practices in neighborhoods nationwide that celebrate the land. Community colleges have plenty of courses and dedicated faculty who struggle to achieve these goals daily. But the immediacy of climate change and its impacts on the landscape, and the lack of national support to fund public education, are real and endangering. Even recommitting to the mission will most likely not be enough.

We also need advocacy that focuses efforts on what these institutions were meant to be and could become: the principal institutions to create greater equity in employment, housing, representation, and quality-of-life issues in America. These changes happen by opening the curriculum: creating new degrees and areas of study focused on specific emerging problems, and making youth in our communities, including those who are incarcerated, change agents of their own neighborhoods and communities.

Any fundamental impact upon the existing system must specifically aim to empower underrepresented and poor communities. Universities and colleges across the globe have found great success launching transdisciplinary collaborations for research and teaching. New nonaccredited professional degrees could offer opportunities. These could include degrees in the uncovering and rethinking of Black landscapes, in urban agriculture innovations, or in every aspect of resilient and green infrastructure neighborhood construction.

For instance, a renewed effort in community-oriented development of housing can be enhanced by two-year degree programs that recognize and legitimize this specific area of inquiry. New associate degrees could reflect empowerment and engagement practices that recognize and reflect a better, more inclusive history of the land as we deal with gentrification effects and increasing informal settlements. Some argue that many do not need to aim for a college degree and should have alternative opportunities following high school. The reality is that the demands of our cities and the climate crisis necessitate that more young people obtain a two-year experience in higher education—not only for adequate incomes but, more importantly, for sustainable living practices. I first began rethinking community colleges a few years ago. Today, free education has become a major campaign issue at the presidential level.

Community colleges could be reinvented to bring landscapes back in focus, making clear that landscapes are all around us in the urban and rural spaces we inhabit. In *What Is Landscape?* Stilgoe links a reference to J. B. Jackson to a search for why landscapes matter: "Looking carefully at landscape over time often raises issues most scholars miss. In subsequent books he [Jackson] angled the field toward what he called 'vernacular' landscape . . . the one made and used by most people most of the time."[69] Stilgoe goes on to add, "In the minds of many Americans, 'landscape' designates . . . something other than *townscape* and especially *cityscape*."[70] Landscape as much signifies how we personally come to something, to a place.

Landscapes matter if we ever intend to comprehend how and why we navigate them. Part of the answer in comprehending landscapes is understanding the power of crossroads in the landscape. Not so much like Africa Road, but more like the veves of Vodun that offer symbolic manifestation of the crossroads, where landscape intersects and collides with African cultural roots and meaning. I see it more plainly where Black landscape architects—young and old, women and men—have defined places and built them to respond as crossroads. Whether Sara Zewde examines the place of African slaves pouring into Brazil, or Charles Fountain, Glenn Smith, Edward Pryce, and Perry Howard navigate paths for future generations, or Elizabeth Kennedy makes Brooklyn reflect and remember, or Kofi Boone holds the modern-day mirror so that others find new ways to speak of their landscapes, there is a little bit of trickster always at work among these guardians of the crossroads.

The Mardi Gras (or Black) Indians demonstrate that one can allow the end destination to inform one's journey through a landscape, celebrating the unpredictability of the path as well as the predictable point of arrival. Knowing that Black landscapes exist allows all of us to contemplate the vast contributions made by African Americans as we move through the unchartered spaces of our future built environments.

Perhaps Hansberry, possibly referring to Washington Park in Chicago, well understood this notion when she wrote:

It is a long time. One forgets the reason for the game. . . . Why was it important to take a small step, a teeny step, or the most desired of all—one giant step?

A giant step to where?...

And, sometimes, when Chicago nights got too steamy, the whole family got into the car and went to the park and slept out in the open on blankets. Those were, of course, the best times of all because the grownups were invariably reminded of having been children in the South and told the best stories then.[71]

Notes

1. Bertrand Butler, Joyce Jackson, and Brenda Marie Osbey, conversations with the author.

2. Butler, Jackson, and Osbey, conversations with the author.

3. *Dave Chappelle: "Equanimity" and "The Bird Revelation,"* directed by Stan Lathan (Netflix, 2017); *Katt Williams: Great America*, directed by Leslie Small, produced by Aaron Latham James, Gerald McBride, Lena Smith, and Katt Williams (Netflix, 2018).

4. Destination Tips, "12 of the Worst Places to Live in the U.S.," YouTube video, posted June 17, 2016, 4:09, www.youtube.com/watch?v=8nGYkEBDjX8.

5. Ira Berlin, *Many Thousands Gone: The First Two Centuries of Slavery in North America* (Cambridge: Belknap Press of Harvard University Press, 1998).

6. Phyl Garland, "Atlanta: Black Mecca of the South," *Ebony,* August 1971.

7. Published annually by African American Victor Hugo Green from 1936 to 1966, *The Negro Motorist Green Book* was a travel guide for African Americans in the United States during the era of Jim Crow segregation laws.

8. *Selma,* directed by Ava DuVernay, produced by Christian Colson, Dede Gardner, Jeremy Kleiner, and Oprah Winfrey (Los Angeles, CA, 2014).

9. John R. Stilgoe, *What Is Landscape?* (Cambridge, MA: MIT Press, 2015), 18.

10. Thomas C. Dent, *Southern Journey: A Return to the Civil Rights Movement* (New York: William Morrow, 1997).

11. *Claiming Open Spaces,* directed and produced by Austin Allen (Columbus, OH: Urban Garden Films, 1995).

12. Café Brasil, a Frenchmen Street landmark, opened in November 1985 as a coffee shop and multipurpose performance venue. It closed its doors in 2006.

13. Dent, *Southern Journey.*

14. Mable Hoskins Oatis, interview by the author, June 29, 2017.

15. Reverdy C. Ransom, *Preface to History of A.M.E. Church* (Nashville, TN: A.M.E. Sunday School Union, 1950), 112.

16. Carl C. Anthony, *The Earth, the City, and the Hidden Narrative of Race* (New York: New Village, 2017).

17. Oatis, interview by the author.

18. Toni Morrison, *Beloved* (New York: Random House, 1987).

19. Octavia E. Butler, *Parable of the Sower* (New York: Seven Stories, 1993).

20. Gloria Naylor, *The Women of Brewster Place* (New York: Penguin, 1983).

21. Teju Cole, *Open City* (New York: Random House, 2011).

22. John Edgar Wideman, *The Homewood Trilogy* (New York: Avon, 2008); John Edgar Wideman, *Fanon* (New York: Houghton Mifflin, 2008), 99.

23. Chester Himes, *If He Hollers Let Him Go* (Cambridge, MA: Da Capo, 1945), 84.

24. Isabel Wilkerson, *The Warmth of Other Suns* (New York: Random House, 2010).

25. Edward Branley, "NOLA History: Congo Square and the Roots of New Orleans Music," *GoNOLA,* July 2, 2012, https://gonola.com/things-to-do-in-new-orleans/arts-culture/nola-history-congo-square-and-the-roots-of-new-orleans-music.

26. Justin Martin, *Genius of Place: The Life of Frederick Law Olmsted* (Cambridge, MA: Da Capo, 2011), 192–95.

27. "St. Katharine Drexel," Catholic Online, www.catholic.org/saints/saint.php?saint_id=193.

28. "Interactive Timeline," Sisters of the Blessed Sacrament, www.katharinedrexel.org/st-katharine-drexel-overview/interactive-timeline/.

29. Cole, *Open City.*

30. Colson Whitehead, *Zone One* (New York: Anchor, 2011); *The Third Man*, directed and produced by Carol Reed (Shepperton, UK, 1949); *Insecure*, produced by Issa Rae (HBO series, 2016–20); *Fleabag*, TV series produced by Phoebe Waller-Bridge (2016–19).

31. Cole, *Open City,* 59.

32. Diana Samuels, "St. George Incorporation Portrayed as 'Secession' in National Media," *New Orleans Times-Picayune,* December 4, 2013.

33. Eric Craig, "New Orleans East Residents, Activists Discuss Secession from City," *New Orleans Times-Picayune,* May 10, 2017.

34. Ron Chernow, *Grant* (New York: Penguin, 2017).

35. Second Peace Conference at The Hague, *Signed—18 October 1907: Entry into Force—26 January 1910: Laws and Customs of War on Land, Article 25.*

36. Sarah McCammon, "The Story behind '40 Acres and a Mule,'" *Code Switch,* NPR, January 12, 2015, audio, 3:44, www.npr.org/sections/codeswitch/2015/01/12/376781165/the-story-behind-40-acres-and-a-mule.

37. McCammon, "The Story behind '40 Acres and a Mule.'"

38. Roberta Brandes Gratz, *The Battle for Gotham: New York in the Shadow of Robert Moses and Jane Jacobs* (New York: Nation, 2010), xix.

39. Richard Sennett, "The Open City, The Closed System: The Brittle City," Urban Age Conference, Berlin, Germany, November 11, 2006, https://urbanage.lsecities.net/essays/the-open-city.

40. Jane Jacobs, *The Death and Life of Great American Cities* (New York: Random House, 1961), 274.

41. Frank S. Horne, "The Open City, Threshold to American Maturity," *Phylon Quarterly* 19, no. 2 (1957): 133–39.

42. Alexander von Hoffman, "Like Fleas on a Tiger? A Brief History of the Open Housing Movement," Joint Center for Housing Studies of Harvard University (August 1998), www.jchs.harvard.edu/sites/default/files/von_hoffman_w98-3.pdf; Arnold R. Hirsch, "'Containment' on the Home Front: Race and Federal Housing Policy from the New Deal to the Cold War," *Journal of Urban History* 26, no. 2 (January 2000): 158–89.

43. Von Hoffman, "Like Fleas on a Tiger?"

44. Arnold R. Hirsch, "'The Last and Most Difficult Barrier': Segregation and Federal Housing Policy in the Eisenhower Administration, 1953–1960," Poverty & Race Research Action Council (2005): 44, www.prrac.org/pdf/hirsch.pdf.

45. Frank S. Horne, "Planning for Public Housing: Under the Public Policy of New York City and State," Women's City Club of New York, December 5, 1956.

46. Karl R. Popper, *The Open Society and Its Enemies* (London: Routledge, 1945).

47. Harold Cruse, *The Crisis of the Negro Intellectual* (New York: William Morrow, 1967), 9.

48. Cruse, *The Crisis of the Negro Intellectual,* 12–14.

49. Kees Christiaanse, "Curating the Open City: An Interview with Kees Christiaanse," *Places,* September 2009, https://placesjournal.org/article/curating-the-open-city/.

50. *The World, The Flesh and the Devil,* directed by Ranald MacDougall, produced by George Englund, Sol C. Siegel, and Harry Belafonte (Los Angeles, CA, 1959).

51. Chernow, *Grant.*

52. Baker Canal Corridor Project, www.bakercanalcorridorproject.com.

53. Steve Hardy, "Engineers Hope to Open Comite River Canal in 2021; Work Isn't Just Digging a 12-Mile Ditch," *Advocate,* November 7, 2018.

54. Ivor van Heerden and Mike Bryan, *The Storm* (New York: Viking, 2006) 80; Douglas Brinkley, *The Great Deluge: Hurricane Katrina, New Orleans, and the Mississippi Gulf Coast* (New York: HarperCollins, 2006), 124.

55. Marc Parry, "How Should We Memorialize Slavery?" *Chronicle of Higher Education,* August 29, 2017.

56. Clark Kerr, *The Uses of the University* (Cambridge, MA: Harvard University Press, 2001); Donna Jean Murch, *Living for the City: Migration, Education, and the Rise of the Black Panther Party in Oakland, California* (Chapel Hill: University of North Carolina Press, 2010), 73–74.

57. Murch, *Living for the City,* 96–116.

58. Marian L. Gade and George Strauss, "In Memoriam: Clark Kerr," University of California Academic Senate, 2003, https://senate.universityofcalifornia.edu/_files/inmemoriam/html/clarkkerr.html; Simon Marginson, *The Dream Is Over: The Crisis of Clark Kerr's California Idea of Higher Education* (Oakland: University of California Press, 2016).

59. Seth Rosenfeld, "The Cautionary Tale of Clark Kerr," *San Francisco Chronicle,* December 4, 2003.

60. Clark Kerr, *The Great Transformation in Higher Education, 1960–1980* (Albany: State University of New York Press, 1991).

61. Clark Kerr, *12 Systems of Higher Education: 6 Decisive Issues,* International Council for Educational Development (New York: Interbook, 1978).

62. Seth Rosenfeld, *Subversives: The FBI's War on Student Radicals, and Reagan's Rise to Power* (New York: Picador, 2013).

63. "History: First Community College," Joliet Junior College, accessed October 14, 2019, www.jjc.edu/about-jjc/history.

64. This designation is extrapolated based upon Kerr's definition of the first three periods in described in his volume *The Great Transformation in Higher Education, 1960–1980.*

65. Kerr, *The Uses of the University.*

66. Lorraine Hansberry, *To Be Young, Gifted and Black* (New York: Signet, 1970), 93.

67. Ralph Ellison, *Invisible Man* (New York: Random House, 1952).

68. Marginson, *The Dream Is Over.*

69. Stilgoe, *What Is Landscape?,* 211.

70. Stilgoe, *What Is Landscape?,* 215.

71. Hansberry, *To Be Young,* 49–50.

RITUAL AND DISPLACEMENT IN NEW ORLEANS

The Photographs of Lewis Watts

Lewis Watts with Walter Hood

Sixteen fictitious characters introduced me to the work of Lew Watts. It was 1992, and I was living in California, in a West Oakland artist's loft. Collecting stories of the people who I encountered daily became ritual. I would describe experiences at the corner liquor store, or the clandestine meetings happening below on the street, those in the backseats of cars and on the sidewalk, or simply the daily life of Twenty-Ninth Street in West Oakland. As I wrote and described the world around me, it became harder for me to design landscapes within this context of African American life, where social reform planning tactics and social cultural rhetoric offered solutions only to fail a community of people in a big way. My neighborhood stood isolated through freeway infrastructure, low-income housing, and the parasitic uses that followed—manifestations of years of racist planning doctrines. The answers that followed built miniparks and playgrounds and community centers. It seemed that the people had been overlooked, homogenized into the clean demographics of the young and the elderly.

This intention was no accident by those who designed these neighborhood spaces—spaces for Black people. As behaviorists, their solutions were based on clear social science and observational studies; they were looking for straightforward metrics and answers. In my view, this strategy seemed foolish. The same metrics had been used before and failed, as exemplified by the current state of the neighborhood. Why would they work again?

I was filled with apathy as I looked at the context in which I lived, and every time I made a drawing or a proposal for a landscape something seemed missing. I stopped utilizing the behaviorist methods I had learned in school and started to think increasingly about culture. Could I design a landscape that was inspired by African American daily life? Could I design a landscape that was inspired by the African American cultural arts?

The park plan for Courtland Creek Park in East Oakland provided a turn for my thinking about language, meaning, and representation of Black landscapes. One evening, at a neighborhood meeting, I presented a plan for the park, unveiling a linear park using the basic landscape architecture toolbox of plan and sections, all rendered nicely with markers and pencils. As I surveyed the all-Black group that gathered that evening, the disconnect was clear. The way I spoke of the park design conveyed nothing to people living for years next to a vacant leftover space, and the images I presented were meaningless.

At that moment I decided to change the language and the representation. Through collage, I constructed nine perspective drawings, highlighting houses and other familiar elements. The drawings were crude—for instance, I showed red trees vividly rendered in oil paste. They conveyed not a pretty homogeneous park, but something different. They included people's lives, and their context. The collages, with black-and-white photos I had shot juxtaposed with the mix of colors, proved arresting. Unknowingly, I was embracing the cultural turn in design and planning. I was seeking ways to bring in new narratives and representations.

Photography, unbeknownst to me, had preceded my thinking in the early 1990s. This was the time at UC Berkeley's College of Environmental Design when photography, drawing, and painting were central to the pedagogy. Lew Watts was part of the Visual Studies program, and, in hindsight, there is no question why I was attracted to his work when I saw it—them—those sixteen fictitious characters. I had seen recent shows by photographers who dealt with Black subject matter, such as Robert Mapplethorpe at BAMF and Carrie Mae Weems at the SFMOMA, and seeing the work of Lew, a colleague, made even deeper impressions on me.

His images forever changed how I look at Black landscape space. Lew's work is at once portraiture and landscape; his eye is keen in capturing a moment, a circumstance, and a person. Armed with my own narratives, his portfolio was familiar to me. I selected sixteen images from Lew's trove of work, and we produced a volume called *Blues & Jazz Landscape Improvisations.* In his portfolio, I looked for the loner, the musician, the poet, the thief, the optimist, the pessimist, the inventor, the cook, the single parent, the anarchist, the apathetic, the lover, the loner, the inventor, the dreamer, and the bureaucrat. They were all there in Lew's photographs.

Lew's work documents Black landscapes, but, more importantly, it documents that we are here, that we were there. It documents the image of the Black body, and the importance of the Black body to how we make space that is inclusive. It documents the image of the Black body not as the spectacle but as the mundane. In this way, we become familiar with the image of the Black male as a person, the Black youth as children who run and play, the Black woman as beautiful, and the elderly as possessing beauty and dignity, people who exist in the same space as everyone else.

—Walter Hood

Government Food on the Levee, River Road, outside of New Orleans. (Lewis Watts, 1994, photograph courtesy of the artist)

Central City, New Orleans. (Lewis Watts, 1995, photograph courtesy of the artist)

LEWIS WATTS WITH WALTER HOOD

RITUAL AND DISPLACEMENT IN NEW ORLEANS   139

Uncle Lionel, Tremé Brass Band.
(Lewis Watts, 2002, photograph
courtesy of the artist)

LEWIS WATTS WITH WALTER HOOD

Wedding Dress in Flooded Area in the Lower 9th Ward, 6 Weeks after Hurricane Katrina. (Lewis Watts, 2005, photograph courtesy of the artist)

St. Claude Avenue, 9th Ward, 6 Weeks after the Storm (Lewis Watts, 2005, photograph courtesy of the artist)

LEWIS WATTS WITH WALTER HOOD

Baptism Bath in Gutted Church, Lower 9th Ward. (Lewis Watts, 2006, photograph courtesy of the artist)

By the Remains of House Built by Her Father, Lower 9th Ward. (Lewis Watts, 2006, photograph courtesy of the artist)

David Montana of the Yellow Pocahontas Tribe and His Aunt, Mardi Gras Day, Tremé. (Lewis Watts, 2007, photograph courtesy of the artist)

LEWIS WATTS WITH WALTER HOOD

"To the Ancestors," Guardian of the Flame Art Society, Harrison Family Home, Upper 9th Ward, Mardi Gras Morning. (Lewis Watts, 2007, photograph courtesy of the artist)

Beads on Tree, Mardi Gras Day, Tremé. (Lewis Watts, 2007, photograph courtesy of the artist)

Celebrating the 9th Ward, 2nd Line Parade. (Lewis Watts, 2008, photograph courtesy of the artist)

LEWIS WATTS WITH WALTER HOOD

Brass Band after Playing for a Funeral Procession, Tremé. (Lewis Watts, 2010, photograph courtesy of the artist)

LEWIS WATTS WITH WALTER HOOD

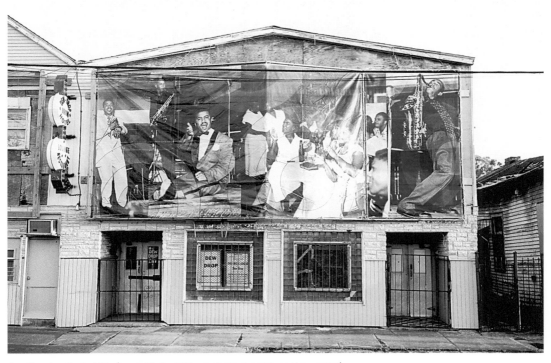

Dew Drop Inn, Central City. (Lewis Watts, 2014, photograph courtesy of the artist)

Anti-Violence Festival, St. Rochs, New Orleans. (Lewis Watts, 2014, photograph courtesy of the artist)

THE BEERLINE TRAIL

Milwaukee, Wisconsin

Sara Daleiden

There is no use wishing it were a simpler problem or trying to make it a simpler problem, because in real life it is not a simpler problem. No matter what you try to do to it, the city park behaves like a problem in organized complexity, and that is what it is.
—Jane Jacobs, *The Death and Life of Great American Cities*

The Black Landscape and Trauma Processing for Cultural Bodies

What is a "Black landscape"? I imagine a "Black landscape" can express the long U.S. history of labor and migration related to race, and the associated lands traveled and cultivated. I imagine a "Black landscape" can invent a public-space commons that acknowledges and celebrates "Black" culture as an integral aesthetic layer of U.S. culture, both now and since its inception. I imagine a "Black landscape" can help define an "ethical cultural development" in a U.S. urban context, investing in existing residents, workers, and others who may migrate to a neighborhood, many of whom associate with "Black" representation. I imagine a "Black landscape" can

2016 aerial view of the Beerline Trail at Burleigh and Bremen Streets facing southeast within the Riverwest neighborhood in Milwaukee. (Photograph by Tim McCollow, courtesy of Sara Daleiden and Tim McCollow)

hold an inspiring and heartwarming cultural exchange with "Black," "white," and any other cultural layer a resident wants to own. And maybe a "Black landscape" is a place that supports neighbors to focus on the civic so we can walk toward freedom from racism and the inequities and trauma it can trigger and produce in any of us.

Through my cultural exchange initiative MKE–LAX, I have been collaborating with Hood Design Studio and local cultural leaders to design landscape and art strategies for a linear park as part of a creative district. We call the project the Beerline Trail Neighborhood Development Project (Beerline Trail Project). The design concerns material aspects—its access ways, infrastructure, and the existing trail—as well as the immaterial: the process and strategies involved in shaping a landscape. In this undertaking, I am aware of the aesthetic tendencies in the United

States surrounding recreational trails, and the history of community development in neighborhoods with significant clusters of residents who associate with "African American" or "Black" representation. A healthy and sustainable model of a "Black landscape," and flexibility around its application, is a time-sensitive cultural innovation needed in the United States.

Every day in Milwaukee, I move between two cities, one stereotypically labeled as "Black Milwaukee" and the other as "white Milwaukee." In working on the Beerline Recreational Trail (Beerline Trail), I directly engage with a geographic border space that holds the residue of racial segregation practices and policies (both legal and illegal). In one Milwaukee, residents and visitors who associate with being "people of color" feel comfortable living, working, and moving in that space, and, in the other Milwaukee, they often do not. People who associate with being "white" in Milwaukee can have the same experience from an inverse geographic perspective. These divergent experiences mean Milwaukee can feel like a constipated city: there is often high anxiety and questionable mobility for residents, regardless of racial representation.

As individuals and as groups, we can guide our governmental bodies to produce a shared cultural body. As city residents, we are often unaware of our contributions that produce this cultural body. Hurdles to awareness include race dynamics in the city, some of which can be attributed to individual and cultural introversion; some to habit, lack of curiosity, unprocessed trauma, or depression; and others to deepset, visible and invisible biases like "white supremacy."

I have been questioned by people from a range of racial associations about why I work in what could be interpreted as a "Black landscape." I can be read by others, and at times by myself, as associated with "white Milwaukee" or as being "white" because of my multiethnic cultural representation of "European American" roots and my upbringing in "small-town" Wisconsin. I will often respond that I work on the culturally sensitive development of a U.S.-American[1] landscape based in a "commons"—a cultural place collaboratively owned, cared for, and activated by a full range of citizens and other residents. I encourage the production of a commons that embraces "African American" or "Black" culture as a major aspect of U.S.-American culture along with many other cultures. I support a commons that acknowledges the often violent civil-rights violations that frequently occur in this country's public spaces.

I enjoy a commons that balances human and nonhuman nature as a cultural development value. I desire a commons that makes room for protest and experiential political expression as important exercises in a healthy democratic practice.

In Milwaukee, when different cultural groups stay in their respective corners of the city, there is no commons. The geographic experience of cultural separation in Milwaukee arises partly from racial segregation, and partly from the civic engagement strategies employed to encourage "integration." The history and current practice of racial segregation and integration is a recurring paradigm in many U.S.-American, often urban, contexts. In Milwaukee, cultural separation can also be attributed to an introverted psyche in the cultural body. The intense long winters have nurtured that introversion over time, and other factors, including current relationships with technology, encourage city residents to interact infrequently or within familiar cultural clusters. Cultural clusters can be a healthy instinct for residents who have an affinity for one another, but, when linked to race dynamics where there is a lack of perceived and actual mobility, civil-rights violations often arise.

The cultural separation, racial segregation, introversion, and related civil-rights violations can stimulate pain and anxiety in any "body" in Milwaukee. It can be considered our trauma. As an antidote to this trauma, the Beerline Trail Project has been implemented as a health and well-being initiative for the neighborhoods and the city. The project provides health and well-being in a physical, social, and spatial sense, at the scale of an individual body and a cultural body. Because our cultural body involves many bodies, we need to make these decisions together, based in trust, however new and unfamiliar the trust may feel.

The Beerline Trail Project is tough for all the reasons that transforming race dynamics in the United States can feel unbearable, and sometimes barely possible. In part, these difficulties emerge from our country's lack of historical honesty around slavery and related racial injustices, and our inability to embrace the aftershocks that continue to reverberate. I have found breathing room within the difficulty, within the playful and serene gathering place of the Beerline Trail, and have witnessed others around me taking similar deep breaths.

As Beerline Trail Project collaborators, we activate the trail to understand a shared cultural body. This cultural body can include the neighbors surrounding the trail and others who want to practice the necessary reciprocal and generative trust and honesty. We strive to carefully craft a productive and respectful process for our individual and cultural traumas, recognizing that complexity, endurance, and resilience are key to our cultural well-being. This process takes time and translation, and the Beerline Trail is a place to begin this cultural exchange. It is a commons where we can walk with each other to make repeatable discoveries around healing and connection.

MKE–LAX Walks the Beerline Trail

I grew up outside the midwestern freshwater port of Milwaukee, in a small town in Wisconsin called Waukesha. I walked all over the town as a way of connecting to my neighbors and my neighborhood. It was in Milwaukee where I learned to become an artist, often walking through the landscape where the Beerline Trail is now located. I migrated to the booming global port city of Los Angeles over a decade ago, prompted by my curiosity and attraction to the extremity of U.S. western landscapes. I often explore Los Angeles through urban hiking, an activity that also aligns with my interests in market access and arts and cultural production. I started MKE–LAX as a way of teaching myself about the production of contemporary U.S.-American culture, picking two geographically separate places within the United States to explore the power dynamic between them and their influences (actual and potential) on each other over time.

As a cultural exchange initiative, MKE–LAX facilitates meaningful interactions among people within these two developing landscapes. The name MKE–LAX refers to the airport codes of Milwaukee and Los Angeles, both cultural epicenters that feed their surrounding regions. My biregional facilitation practice brings artists and other cultural workers from each place to the other, exploring cultural exchange between them through residencies, public programs, development projects, and other place-based initiatives. Using cultural exchange strategies exercised among people from different countries, I intend to grow a mutual understanding between U.S. regions and their residents. My approach to cultural exchange is based in listen-

Neighborhood children play on the recreational trail as part of the On the Trail Designer Experience at the Beerline Trail extension in the Harambee neighborhood in Milwaukee in 2016. (Photograph by Adam Carr, courtesy of Sara Daleiden and the Greater Milwaukee Committee)

ing and walking, the use of my body and my presence, and my capacity for a range of nonverbal and verbal communication to share knowledge and experience among cultures.

I use elements of this strategy to approach the Beerline Trail Project, one focus within MKE–LAX. As one of the core cultural leaders of the project, I work with Hood Design Studio, the cultural leadership network on the ground, and others across various sectors to foster equitable development values. The Beerline Trail Project is comprised of the City of Milwaukee, Greater Milwaukee Committee (GMC), Local Initiatives Support Corporation (LISC), MKE–LAX, and Riverworks Development Corporation and Riverworks Business Improvement District (Riverworks).[2]

Tendencies I cultivate in Los Angeles and nationally are evident in my work with the Beerline Trail Project: those of public art, civic art, social practice art, creative placemaking, landscape architecture, and urban design. I emphasize equity and inclusive communications. I incorporate other methods for engaging with cultural geography, often focusing on the pedestrian experience. I approach this work in Milwaukee as a time-sensitive conversation that navigates race dynamics and cultural production within Milwaukee and the entire United States. It is based in the desire for self-determined mobility for all residents, whether mobility as pedestrians, as citizens, as workers, or as whatever other cultural representation residents find desirable to embrace for themselves.

In this context, we explore what collaboration and agency can feel like through growing a new public space based in the arts. We create arts-centric civic gathering spaces; we invest in cultural exchange for existing and incoming cultures. We conceive of a city as a trail network, and prioritize pedestrians and bicyclists. In a city built for cars and industry, we facilitate walking, biking, and other engagement on the trail to accentuate human interaction.

To encourage construction of this well-loved commons that I envision, I start by accepting the myriad layers of trauma, ignorance, experimentation, and possibility upon the land where I was born and raised. Most days in Milwaukee, I code-switch all day long. By "code-switch," I mean that I adjust my representation and language to respond to the active power dynamics and other cultural negotiations of my context. In doing so, my voice and my presence, and those of others, are more likely to be acknowledged within a place. With cultural development projects like the Beerline Trail Project, I code-switch to create physical and social contexts for neighbors who often recognize each other as having different racial representations. I strive for a context where neighbors can explore extreme feelings of separation from each other, even as they share neighborhoods.

It is these adjacent neighborhoods and shared spaces to which I turn. To address the race dynamics that are felt easily throughout Milwaukee and its developing landscapes, it is useful to focus on a border space shared by the neighborhoods. In the instance explored here, this border includes the public space of the Beerline Trail. The Beerline Trail Project has grown from our development of the Beerline Trail, initiated in 2002, and Creational Trails: The ARTery, initiated in 2012. In 2014, inspired by this previous work on the trail, the Beerline Trail Project's creative placemaking collaboration formalized to mobilize neighborhood stakeholders in the Riverworks area, specifically the Harambee and Riverwest neighborhoods.

From Rail to Trail with the Beerline

The development of the Beerline Trail has come to steer an emotional public conversation around racial equity and its consequent effects on the lived experience of Milwaukeeans. Located on a piece of land formerly home to the Beerline rail line and its Gibson Yards rail yard, this site was part of the infamous beer industry's distribution system and has grown into a trail and linear park. Our work at the site has been stimulated through creative placemaking grants from national foundations, including ArtPlace America and the Kresge Foundation, who are affecting inclusive development in disinvested areas typical to U.S.-American cities like the Beerline Trail Project area.[3] These grants have primarily come through a citywide community development nonprofit organization called the Greater Milwaukee Committee (GMC), a CEO leadership group in existence since the 1940s. As a civic advocacy organization, the GMC focuses on economic prosperity, talent and innovation, and vibrancy of place. The history of manufacturing beer, automobiles, machine parts, leather, and other products in Milwaukee—industries that are still somewhat active—is a key layer of the Beerline Trail Project, as the warehouses that line the trail often have daily commercial use.

In developing the trail with the City of Milwaukee Department of Public Works (DPW), we found that some of the land was an industrial brownfield in need of a remediation strategy. Part of my collaborative work supported DPW in activating their plan, and used the allotted federal and state Department of Transportation (DOT) funding to buy the property and install the trail extension in the rail yard.

The Beerline Trail's initial development phase started in 2002. To actualize this section, an array of cross-sector partnerships was needed. The historic Beerline rail line had begun as a rails-to-trails project through the DPW, the River Revitalization Foundation, Riverworks, and other neighborhood leaders with support from the State of Wisconsin DOT and other local funders. In 2007, the initial Beerline Trail segment opened, and the Beerline Trail extension in Harambee opened in 2015. Though owned by the DPW, the Beerline Trail remains collaboratively managed by Riverworks and other neighborhood leaders.

Through development of this Beerline Trail commons, we have created a microclimate of a democratic practice often difficult to produce in the United States. We continue to navigate the race dynamics within our project and city leadership as we make decisions together. As of 2015, there is a ten-foot-wide asphalt path extension for biking, skateboarding, walking, and other commuting and recreational activities, as well as a simple array of native plantings. With Hood Design Studio, we are presently developing wayfinding and other connectivity measures that are meaningful for active use—as well as reimagining what more can be physically and socially present in this new commons.

Connecting Neighbors of the Beerline Trail

As mentioned, two of the core neighborhoods involved with the Beerline Project are Harambee and Riverwest. The two neighborhoods share a border called Holton Street, a major north-south transportation corridor for the city. The Beerline Trail diagonally crosses Holton Street, serving as a bridge and a "third space" that connects the two neighborhoods. Harambee, the neighborhood west of Holton Street, forms the eastern edge of a series of neighborhoods called the "Northside" of Milwaukee. Its population often associates with being "African American" and "people of color." The residents of Riverwest, the neighborhood east of Holton Street, are a broad mix of racial representations and classes, partly due to proximity to a state university that attracts a range of cultures from within Wisconsin and beyond.

Historic racial segregation in the city can be traced to the significant edge created by Holton Street. Banks, government, and other financial and legal power brokers set parameters for where "African American" residents or other "people of color" could own property and live. Segregation residue is still actively experienced on Holton Street and in the neighborhoods, and "African American" residents often navigate generations of poverty and other challenges that can easily emerge from the historic and present racial segregation. Residents and workers within both neigh-

Focus area map for the Beerline Trail Neighborhood Development Project in Milwaukee, as of 2018. (Map courtesy of Hood Design Studio)

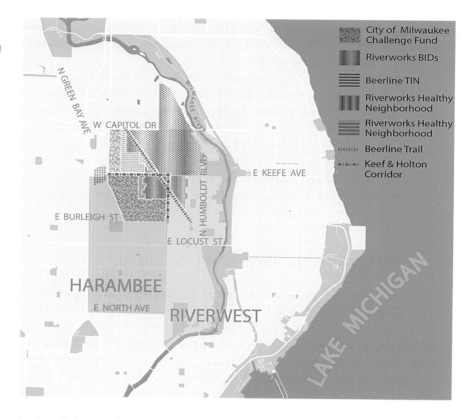

borhoods frequently express concerns about crime and other tensions among neighbors, and note Holton Street as a border zone.

In the 1950s, the construction of Interstate 43 through the "Northside" (the west edge of Harambee) disrupted many historically "African American" neighborhoods. Like Harambee, these neighborhoods were composed of a range of classes. They included a healthy middle class of factory workers who had migrated as extended families from Mississippi and Alabama to own homes and work for a sustainable living wage in the North.

American Motors Corporation (AMC) was one of the major businesses in the

Riverworks district. Since its closure in the 1980s, there has been significant poverty in the area, exacerbated by the recession in the 2000s. Presently, many residents who formerly worked in the nearby businesses are unemployed, or are not employed in the Riverworks district or nearby neighborhoods. A strong disconnect can exist among the residences and businesses that had once grown together. Many current business owners live far from the area. Warehouses that historically employed thousands of workers might now have fifty or fewer. Although there are not many vacant warehouses, underutilized industrial space is common.

Amid this paradigm exists a strong history and current practice of community organizing in both neighborhoods. Community organizing can include formal and informal efforts including nonprofit organizations, business and neighborhood improvement districts, neighborhood associations, safety taskforces, block clubs, cooperatives, community gardens, and markets. These social justice forms encourage agency and economic opportunities for neighbors within a complicated cultural geography.

The industrial creative district known as Riverworks[4] overlays the two neighborhoods of Harambee and Riverwest and other neighborhoods bordering them. The district has grown as a creative district in recent years; its base of small businesses continues to increase and thrive with formal and informal trade in the warehouses and houses, and diverse creative entrepreneurship includes art, design, crafts, food, and more. The Beerline Trail Project collaborators and I have experimented here: investigating how indoor and outdoor marketplaces can support these creative entrepreneurs, and how to offer support to small businesses through Wisconsin Women Business Initiative Corporation (WWBIC) and other local resources. Support allows entrepreneurs to stabilize and expand in tandem with further development of the trail.

Our collaborative efforts along the Beerline Trail have focused on connecting the pastoral Milwaukee River, which forms the east edge of Riverwest, and the city's impressive freshwater body, Lake Michigan. Some youth have never visited the lake, perceiving it as inaccessible, sometimes due to safety concerns from being read as "African American" on the city's "Eastside." The Beerline Trail is part of a growing regional trail network in and around Milwaukee, and though it has many easy access points to the southeast, there is limited access to the northwest. Moving forward, partly through alignment with the national nonprofit Rails to Trails' "Route of the Badger" project for Southeastern Wisconsin, our efforts advocate for the northwest extension of the Beerline Trail. The extension will strengthen connections to the north and west into a neighboring city (along the historic highway of Capitol Drive), and develop multiple access ways to the trail. One milestone in our process has opened access to pedestrians on the north end of the trail extension, allowing residents to cross a bridge over the heavily trafficked Capitol Drive to reach retail and other services.

Reimagining Land from Private to Public with the ARTery

Reimagining a former rail yard into a public space is an ambitious act, especially when the former rail yard can be perceived as a back alley of the internalized industrial warehouses that line the trail. Yet, the place's unusual openness from recent decades as a long and underused border space was advantageous when rescripting a landscape for residents, business owners, and workers with varying racial and other cultural representations, and who often do not share public space elsewhere in the city.

The effort to reconceptualize the former rail yard started as a temporary set of art-based performances, installations, workshops, and other cultural forms called Creational Trails: The ARTery at the Beerline Recreational Trail Extension. Founded by beINtween, in 2012, and developed as a collaboration among local cultural leadership,[5] the ARTery has been a community-driven process for defining public space. It has also been an alternative name for, in this case, transforming the private land of the former rail yard into the public land extension of the Beerline Trail.

Through the experimental process of the ARTery, we offered a call for performance ideas to neighbors to explore public space activities. We received responses from professional performers to "amateurs." We asked this broad range of performers to translate their actions from their homes, their streets, their art and cultural centers, and elsewhere in their neighborhood into the unfamiliar space of the trail. We understood that many neighbors often felt hesitant in public space because they identified as "African American" or as "people of color" and thus felt the accompanying safety issues that can easily arise among police and others. We asked ourselves what, exactly, would support these neighbors to share space together publicly. We built stages and other learning and gathering spaces from recycled industrial material, such as shipping containers and railroad ties, acquired from the Port of Milwaukee and other sites. Performance showcase days were held, mixing up the different types of performance. Other days were filled with informal rehearsal and play. All these outgrowths revealed the plethora of existing talent in the surrounding neighborhoods that simply needed a place to be exercised and enjoyed.

From that first season of activity, we grew a complex neighborhood development project—all based in the growth of a linear park as an arts and cultural spine. Subsequent seasons of arts-focused activities harnessed the learnings of the ARTery and the network that formed that first season, and have since continued to flourish.

Wrapping around a Trail with Equitable Development

The equity intention of the Beerline Trail Project promotes health, well-being, and prosperity through increased circulation of resources, voices, ideas, labor, and creativity among people currently living and working in these neighborhoods. Working from this premise, I muse about what culturally sensitive equitable development means in relationship to a trail. I consider how our trail can be interpreted by different neighbors. A recreational biking and walking trail in an industrial landscape can be read within an aesthetic language, prevalent in the United States and abroad, whose cultural tone can be easily associated with "white" culture. This type of trail investment can also be interpreted as a stepping-stone to a type of gentrification that can displace current neighbors from their residences and businesses. A trail can be viewed as a privileged space because of the assumed safety by certain users who may not be profiled by police—or others—because of racial representation. It can be seen as a privileged space because of the assumed economic advantage of owning a bicycle and having recreational time to use the trail. But a trail can also be a comfortable commuter space for biking and walking, in addition to a recreational space.

Around the former rail yard that is the Beerline Trail extension, many residents and workers who associate with being "African American" or "people of color" also associate with coming from a lineage of industrial workers involved with the original rail line and surrounding warehouses. Using the trail to explore a "Black landscape," I wonder how our collaborative efforts can respect this history of labor and migration related to the rail line, as well as current tendencies with the formal and informal labor of our neighbors in the houses and warehouses around the trail. It is especially important when understanding a creative district and its growing entrepreneurial culture, which, in this industrial zone, has the potential to displace current residents, business owners, and workers if respectful measures are not implemented. How can we make a major investment to advance a new public space that prioritizes equitable development and avoids displacement as trail use and related real estate development amplifies?

With the Beerline Trail Project, our collaboration has invested in a new large-scale public space as a commitment to health and well-being for the "Northside" of Milwaukee and the entire city. We recognize the need to address neighborhood development that wraps around the trail. This development involves real estate, but it also involves other forms of economic and cultural development such as supporting creative entrepreneurs; artist-led neighbor engagement actions; and "storybuilding," which refers to the media produced by local artists and other cultural workers that grow the experience and perception of the place. We work with the classic Milwaukee Craftsman–style housing stock to rehabilitate foreclosures, encourage property ownership by longtime neighbors, and support existing property repairs so property owners may stay in place, particularly elder residents. As we fundraise for design and implementation of the linear park, we define how to build and support a long-term equitable development plan, including legal and financial mechanisms that protect current property owners and renters, and a stewardship endowment for maintenance, governance, and programming related to the trail.

Exploring Inclusive Communication through Cultural Exchange

One of the ways we practice equity is through inclusive communication that is inviting and transparent to the broad range of neighbors and civic leaders in the area. This communication encourages creative entrepreneurship, landscape design, neighbor engagement, and stewardship. Using a word like "inclusive" to describe intentions around communicating, relating, and power is complicated, and finding language that resonates locally is part of our work.

As cultural leaders of the Beerline Trail Project, we actively self-reflect about how we communicate. Often, we use the practices of local artists and cultural workers to experiment with different ways of communicating. We also investigate other places where communication can occur. Sometimes people prefer different means of communication—some neighbors prefer a flyer at their front door and others a tweet on their cell phone—because of generational, racial, or other cultural representational reasons. In our communication efforts, we have sensitivity to the perspectives of many neighbors who may not imagine development of a neighborhood park, and whose primary concerns often include having sustainable income, as well as how their neighborhood can heal and grow as they continue to live and work there.

In Milwaukee, it can feel like a radical experience to imagine options, share perspectives, and make decisions within a leadership group that is a mix of races, genders, generations, and other cultural layers. We explore models for gathering people together for intensive periods of time to create a social arch that can encourage feelings of connection among neighbors. For instance, the two-day Strategic Actioning Session in 2015, cofacilitated with Marble Leadership, gathered a range of neighbors and civic leaders with a mix of identities. We asked each neighbor what they valued in their neighborhood or within the Beerline Trail, and what leadership role they desired for themselves. Creative activities were used to conceptualize a cross-sector neighborhood leadership group that we called the Guiding Lenses Group. We curated conversations to mix neighbors in pairs or small groups. In all cases, labor and intention was necessary to make cultural exchange happen successfully.

When I work amid neighbors who often experience significant cultural difference, I use principles learned working with nonnative English speakers from other countries. I emphasize that we must take extra time to communicate—both verbally and nonverbally. We cannot assume we understand, even if we think we all speak the same English language. Translation, though laborious, is often necessary every time we meet. Committing quality time to one another allows for a conversation around race and other cultural sensitivities in which a range of voices can be more easily heard, and we can then meaningfully discuss development questions. This cultural exchange is practiced within the Guiding Lenses Group, but we also apply it in other facilitated contexts such as those we initiate with various departments of the city government.

I strive to generate a context for this type of cultural exchange in Milwaukee, and one way is by identifying and supporting emerging cultural leadership for the Beerline Trail Project. I often start with artists and other cultural workers, many of whom associate with being "Artists of Color" and with hip-hop culture. Many already exercise their artistic voices in connection with their social justice concerns. They are open to exploring decision-making roles to better understand and influence the power dynamics around them—power dynamics that can feel inaccessible and unwieldy but also sometimes hopeful. With my Beerline Trail Project collaborators, I build from existing development initiatives, which in time can be owned by a younger, local generation because we include them in the development discussion now. This younger generation often comprises residents and workers involved in unsanctioned and informal actions of their own invention, sometimes connected to the older generations. These efforts, such as those stemming from Creational Trails, bring vibrancy and health to neighborhoods: the resulting performances, graphics, gardens, workshops, cleanups, spaces, and meetings enable art and culture to self-organize and express in the neighborhoods. Often there is interest from these emerging cultural leaders to learn how to sustain their discoveries and affect the overall culture in Milwaukee.

Cultural Development Model for Working and Playing Together

In my work over the last decade in Los Angeles and in Milwaukee, as I have grown interest in a sustainable model, I have reflected on the cultural and individual traumas in these places related to the concept of a "Black landscape." Processing trauma from racism and other civil rights violations, including the many types of related body violence that can produce the trauma, is embedded within my cultural exchange instincts. While listening and walking are parts of my trauma-processing method, I am also alert to the role of play in my practice. Play as it relates to recreation can, however, be a loaded concept when discussing public space design in neighborhoods where having a livable income and consistent personal safety are daily challenges.

Nonetheless, when I reflect on the successes of the Beerline Trail Project, I sense that to understand our individual and cultural sensitivities, we must discover how to play with each other. Doing so allows us to find trust amid our tensions and ideas. It enables us to look for new ways to define work in relationship to the trail's neighborhoods, understanding the ways we do and do not function as an industrial city. Playing with a sense of agency, comfort, and connection is a pivotal action for this redefinition of work.

I have witnessed many playful moments on the trail, such as children building their own small world on the path as bicyclists and walkers pass by. In creatively claiming space for their play here, these children model that the Beerline Trail is a flexible place for many definitions of work and play, and, subsequently, culture.

Landscapes and Equity

The Beerline Trail Project reinforces that the space and concept of landscape can be a device for practicing racial equity. Through a dedicated practice of racial equity, including decisions involving landscape architecture, an experiment of U.S.-American culture can emerge so that equity in many shapes infuses the experience of our cities.

I look for a landscape experience when I want to stimulate the systems-thinking capacity of my imagination. I look for this experience as I engage with complexity, such as before I make a decision or suggest a recommendation. Landscape experiences can help me as I approach relationships I care about, like the system of public space in Milwaukee.

I walk in the cities I call home, both Milwaukee and Los Angeles, often for an hour or more each day. I walk until my consciousness feels activated—until I can sense what I cannot digest in a single view, a single voice, or a single angle. Moving through landscape is a way to embody the understanding that complexity requires a length of time and space to be read. This requirement can be true for a person, a city, a culture, or a system: all of these exemplify complexity if I allow for that perception.

I accept that to have respectful and generative relationships within U.S.-American culture, regardless the scale of relationship, we must make time and space for complexity around our race dynamics. In the United States, so many erratic influences divert our attention and prevent us from embracing complexity. Too readily, we make choices that separate us into simplistic, but powerful, silos. These silos, however, can evolve to become permeable, so we overlap and blend while still respecting each other's cultures of origin and preferences. Racially based silos are sometimes the most challenging to read consistently; reading them requires the emotional labor of moving through the deep anxiety that built the silos and keeps them in place.

I have been compelled to collaboratively make the Beerline Trail a place for walking and other activities of work, play, and hybrids of the two, and for making time and space to read Milwaukee as a landscape text. A text that we continue to rewrite conscious of the racial complexity within our shared cultural body, and with an enduring intention of equity for all bodies. I embrace the collaboration of the Beerline Trail Project as an experiment in building a "Black landscape."

Notes

1. Because my practice frequently engages with Latina/o, Latin American, and Native American (American Indian or First Nation) cultures, I have become sensitized to the fact that "American" is a difficult term to use when referring to the United States as it can be used for any resident of the Americas, from the North or South continents. I also find "U.S." to not be a rich enough acronym for the "United States of America," as there can be other global contexts that refer to themselves as "united states." Thus, "U.S.-American" is my present solution to describe this nationality I associate with and primarily live and work within.

2. Additional collaborators include the Bader Foundation, Greater Milwaukee Foundation (GMF), Rails to Trails, Wisconsin Women's Business Initiative Corporation (WWBIC), and the Guiding Lenses Group, as well as a range of cultural leaders from the neighborhoods and the city.

3. This project is also supported with local and national resources from the Bader Foundation; CarMax Foundation; City of Milwaukee; Fund for Lake Michigan; GMC; GMF; LISC;

MKE–LAX; National Endowment for the Arts; Office of Community Services; Prairie Springs: Paul Fleckenstein Trust; Riverworks; Transform Milwaukee; WWBIC; Zilber Foundation; and other donors.

4. Riverworks is the name of the creative district. Riverworks also refers to the previously mentioned Riverworks Business Improvement District (BID) and Riverworks Development Corporation (RDC), two agencies that work closely together and are major neighborhood partners of the Beerline Trail Project.

5. beINtween, the Greater Milwaukee Committee, Riverworks Center, the City of Milwaukee, MKE –LAX, and other cultural leaders.

AFTERWORD

Walter Hood

After the Egyptian and the Indian, the Greek and Roman, the Teuton and Mongolian, the Negro is a sort of seventh son, born with a veil, and gifted with second-sight in this American world,—a world which yields him no true self-consciousness, but only lets him see himself through the revelation of the other world. It is a peculiar sensation, this double-consciousness, this sense of always looking at one's self through the eyes of others, of measuring one's soul by the tape of a world that looks on in amused contempt and pity. One ever feels his two-ness,—an American, a Negro; two souls, two thoughts, two unreconciled strivings; two warring ideals in one dark body, whose dogged strength alone keeps it from being torn asunder.
—W. E. B. Du Bois, *The Souls of Black Folk*

E pluribus unum: out of many people with diverse backgrounds, we become one through the acceptance and implementation of the U.S. Constitution, of its claim that all are created equal. The phrase reminds us that Blacks have been present in the landscape since its colonial beginning, offering expertise and talents that shaped a landscape's economy, form, and aesthetic. From the agrarian to the urban, from Louisiana to North and South Carolina, and from Detroit to Milwaukee, these es-

says have explored the Black diaspora that has shaped landscapes and the patterns and practices of those who dwell in them. The cultivation expertise and other skills and technical knowledge learned through acculturation have produced vernacular Black landscape designers, architects, and builders for the landscapes and buildings that we have assumed and credit to white culture.

These essays remind us that the American landscape is a product of its colonial institutions and practices that have never been reconciled and resolved. At this country's core looms the legacy of slavery and the insipid evocations that emerge over time in all parts of our society. These essays also remind us that, if we are not careful, nostalgia can set in and make what we choose to bring back benign, as noted by David Lowenthal: "But it is not simply nostalgia that makes the past powerful. Hindsight and overview enable us to comprehend past environments in ways that elude us when we deal with the shifting present. Because they seem more comprehensible, images from the past often dominate or may wholly replace the present."[1]

But once we document, where do we go from there? Black landscapes have come to light; why have they not mattered to the American narrative? Is it because of their "oneness," or exclusivity, and the narrow cultural interpretations? Is it that others cannot see or understand the connection with them? Or maybe these landscapes have not mattered because, although they unearth, exhume, and uncover lost relics and memories of Black culture, they are tied to an ugly and unforgivable memory.

Is it possible within the marginalized and excluded to see a means for true difference and diversity within the United States? Imagine if we flipped the script on Du Bois's idea of double consciousness: What if we learned from the oppressed and marginalized how to operate within a diverse society? What if we didn't wait for acculturation and appropriation of certain patterns and practices to emerge anew for popular consumption? What if we all had to engage in "looking at ourselves through the eyes of others"? This empathy maybe would allow us to remember, to reconcile, and to create a new history with diverse narratives that elucidate our real strengths and obligations toward one another. I am reminded of Michelle Obama's words: "I wake up every morning in a house that was built by slaves." She, descendant of slaves, residing in the White House, lives with a double consciousness—she must read spaces and places with multiple meanings.

Only those people who live within the double have a way to construct an aesthetic of truth. In the United States, we live under *e pluribus unum*. It is impossible, however, to have oneness. All Americans can learn from people who have had to look at themselves with a two-ness. People should see that they themselves, and landscapes, have multiplicities: we should be moving through space that constantly reminds us that women are equal, that we owe responsibility to natives who were here beforehand, that Black hands built our landscape. Having landscapes with multiplicities forces us not to reconcile, to see that maybe all these forces are irreconcilable—and that is okay.

Elements in the landscape are needed so all people can see reflections of themselves, like memories and mythologies embedded in places that highlight the two-ness. These places have been documented for centuries, as evidenced in maps, journals, and documentation bearing their names and place, yet they did not matter to our country's collective memory.

New narratives are emerging in places such as Monticello; the National Memorial for Peace and Justice in Montgomery, Alabama; and Gadsden's Wharf in Charleston, South Carolina. Through the experience of these places, not only memories are imbued, but so is another consciousness. These three landscapes offer us the opportunity to deal with our obligation toward enslavement, celebrate the vernacular and idiosyncratic, and enable the landscape to be about two or more unreconciled facets.

Arriving at the summit of Monticello, Thomas Jefferson's home that operated on the backs of slave labor, you notice two newly constructed buildings along the southern allée adjacent to the main house. These constructions along the allée, called Mulberry Row, are part of a new pedagogical interpretation: the slave landscape of Monticello. Recent archaeology has also restored the kitchen and living spaces, adjacent to Jefferson's original pavilion, that correspond to Mulberry Row. Visitors tour the housing of Jefferson's extramarital family, learning of their relationship to Jefferson—and particularly the relationship between Jefferson and Sally Hemings.

Standing on that summit, overlooking this picturesque landscape, you are struck by the complexity of the situation. Here, one of the founders of the country has created an architecture and landscape made by the hands of Black slaves that will influence the formal and aesthetic character of the federal architecture, while also fathering children with one of his slaves. What is most notable of this "double" situation is that Jefferson does not hide his relationship with his enslaved population and his enslaved mistress. The slave cabins and kitchen areas sit in plain view, not subserviently, like most do on plantation landscapes, situated far from the main house. Mulberry Row is a landscape of enslavement adjacent to Jefferson's neoclassical Monticello. The duality forces us to look at the landscape through a different and significant lens. White and Black people alike cannot leave Monticello without feeling the impact of a double consciousness—what we feel any time we are seen and defined through the eyes of others. For the first time at Monticello, the visitor experiences a reciprocal view, one that is Black.

This pervasiveness of double consciousness also surrounds the National Memorial for Peace and Justice in Montgomery, Alabama. Bryan Stevenson, one of the project's directors, argues that racial injustice in the United States "casts a shadow across the American landscape" that "cannot be lifted until we shine the light of truth on the destructive violence that shaped our nation, traumatized people of color, and compromised our commitment to the rule of law and to equal justice."[2] It is our obligation to cast light upon this shadow. The memorial forces all visitors to contemplate the duality in "all men are created equal" and the realization that hanging Black people from trees to their death was once a sport for white communities. This contemplation will happen in their communities as dirt from places across the United States will be registered at the memorial along with a hanging pylon, only relocated in situ when accepted by their respective original sites, places in the ordinary landscape in communities across the country. It is significant to this double that this place in Alabama is only the beginning of reconciliation. The new narrative can create a new consciousness in the places where these events happened.

In Charleston, South Carolina, next to the city's aquarium along the southern waterfront, a lawn and walkway gently slope down between two high-rise condominiums. This space is the site of Gadsden's Wharf, the place where it is believed that at least 40 percent of the African diaspora landed, died, and were sold. In 2014, an archaeology report uncovered remnants of the wharf and the storehouse. Yet, in years past, a proposal to build a museum on a site across the street from the aquarium for an international African American museum ironically did not mention Gadsden's Wharf.

Historian Robert MacDonald's 2014 article "Power of Place: Gadsden's Wharf and American History" clearly documents the site and the atrocities that took place there. The site became the touchstone: the obligation for the new siting of the museum and for the evocation of a larger narrative. But at its site this narrative remains unresolved—Gadsden's Wharf, one of the largest in North America at its time, with only a small portion existing today unbuilt, this small sloping lawn between two condos. Within the maritime landscape and constant tourist activity, a museum will stand at this hallowed place, changing the narrative of this vernacular landscape.

One day while our design team conducted a site visit, a resident walking her dog inquired why we were looking around. When we informed her of the project, she seemed genuinely curious and interested.

After this casual meeting, I wondered how the resident, who was white, had returned home and dealt with this new revelation. Now, every day walking her dog, she had to think about the atrocities that took place on her little piece of lawn. Maybe this did not faze her, or she simply forgot, like it is easy to do in place like Charleston where the Black history has been codified in the colonial story to the point of being benign. I wonder how she and others may deal with the double when it is physical and social in the form of a building and a new landscape that presents a new site narrative, and one that will attract Black people from all over the country searching for their "place to sit and think about 'our ancestors.'"[3]

Black landscapes force us to reconsider what is vernacular, and to inculcate the typically narrow, normative interpretations with broader understandings that reflect more complex landscapes, spaces, and objects. Through acculturation, vernacular patterns and practices are shared in distinct places, and should not be confused with stereotypical social patterns of use, such as vibrant street life and celebratory events. These shared and celebrated vernacular landscapes have multiple narratives and have produced distinct physical environments. This multiplicity can be seen in the iron and bricks of New Orleans, Savannah, and Charleston; worker housing in Houston and Washington, DC; and the eight linear miles of suburbs in Detroit. Akin to the acculturation process that happens in music, fashion, and culinary arts, these landscapes are reshaped to present something new out of the old and familiar.

Notes

1. David Lowenthal, "Past Time, Present Place: Landscape and Memory," *Geographical Review* 65, no. 1 (January 1975): 7, https://doi.org/10.2307/213831.

2. "The National Memorial for Peace and Justice," Equal Justice Initiative, February 28, 2018, https://eji.org/national-lynching-memorial.

3. Gracie Bonds Staples, "Atlanta Literary Society Dedicates Toni Morrison 'Bench by the Road,'" *Atlanta Journal-Constitution,* March 8, 2016, www.myajc.com/lifestyles/atlanta-literary-society-dedicates-toni-morrison-bench-the-road/gvga31y94bqfQ6sWrOVKjM/.

CONTRIBUTORS

Austin Allen is an Associate Professor of Practice at the School of Architecture at the University of Texas at Arlington, and a principal at DesignJones LLC. He was an Associate Professor in the Robert Reich School of Landscape Architecture at Louisiana State University from 2010 until 2017, after serving as its inaugural Bickham Chair in 2009. His interests include the recovery and regeneration of landscapes; urbanism, particularly concerning open and just cities; public space; film and media arts; and African American and Caribbean cultural landscapes. Allen is also a two-term member of the LSU Faculty Senate.

He was an Associate Professor of Film and Communication at Cleveland State University, and an Associate Professor of Landscape Architecture at the University of Colorado, Denver. He has been active in recovery projects in New Orleans since 2005, particularly in the Lower Ninth Ward and the Bayou Bienvenue Wetlands Triangle, working with the community on planning, funding, and administration, linking neighborhoods to wetlands and water management. His focus has also been to take lessons learned from New Orleans recovery to the Historic District of Jacmel, Haiti, including work with the Haiti/New Orleans Cultural Task Force. Allen was part of the landscape architecture team of the HUD/DOT Livable Claiborne Communities study for the City of New Orleans 2012/2013. Along with colleagues from Southern University, he conducted research on the Baker Canal Corridor Project. He was also part of the 2009 American Society of Landscape Architects (ASLA) award-winning team for the Rockefeller Park, Strategic Master Plan, Cleveland, Ohio, providing community engagement. DesignJones LLC received the ASLA Medal of Honor for Community Service in October 2016. He and partner, Diane Jones Allen, are also listed as Alumni of the Year for 2017, College of Environmental Design, University of California, Berkeley.

Kofi Boone, ASLA, is a Professor of Landscape Architecture at NC State University in the College of Design. Boone's work is at the overlap between landscape architecture and environmental justice with specializations in democratic design, digital media, and interpreting cultural landscapes. His teaching and professional work have earned numerous awards, including student and professional ASLA awards. He serves on the Board of Directors of both the Conservation Network and the Landscape Architecture Foundation, where he also serves as the Vice President of Education. He is a frequent speaker at national conferences and events. His published work is broadly disseminated in peer-reviewed and popular media, and he is a regular contributor to *Landscape Architecture Magazine.*

Dr. Anna Livia Brand is an Assistant Professor of Landscape Architecture & Environmental Planning at the University of California, Berkeley. Her research focuses on the intersection of race and space, specifically looking at historic Black mecca neighborhoods and how they change through processes of redevelopment and resistance. Her comparative research focuses on cities in the American North and South, including New Orleans, Houston, Atlanta, Chicago, and New York. This work highlights the ongoing spatial impacts and shifting spatial logics of racial processes, while simultaneously tracing resistance to these processes over time. Within this work, she is concerned with the role that urban planning and design might play in liberatory geographies. Dr. Brand is captivated by everyday landscapes and built environments, the materiality and local geography that supports and sustains us. She is interested in the ways that people shape and create a place for themselves and the ways that they imagine more socially just places and communities.

Dr. Brand's background is in urban planning and design, and she has worked professionally as both a planner and designer. She lives with her two sons, Luka and Artie, in the San Francisco Bay Area.

Maurice Cox is currently the Commissioner of Planning and Development for the City of Chicago after serving as the City of Detroit's Director of Planning and Development from May 2015 to September 2019. He has received national acclaim for his ability to incorporate active citizen participation into the design process while achieving the highest quality of design excellence. *Fast Company Magazine* named him one of America's "20 Masters of Design" for his practice of "democratic design." Prior to moving to Michigan, he was Director of Tulane City Center and Associate Dean for Community Engagement at the Tulane University School of Architecture in New Orleans. A cofounder of the national Social Economic Environmental Design (SEED) Network, Cox served as design director of the National Endowment for the Arts (NEA) in Washington, DC, from 2007 to 2010. In that capacity, he led the Mayor's Institute on City Design and the Governor's Institute on Community Design, and oversaw the award of more than two million dollars per year in NEA design grants across the United States. Cox served on the faculty of the School of Architecture at the University of Virginia, as city council member, and mayor of the City of Charlottesville from 1996 to 2004. During his mayoral term, the city was ranked as the "#1 Best Place to Live in the USA & Canada" by *Frommer's* "Cities Ranked and Rated" and was also the smallest city in America to maintain an AAA-bond rating for excellence in fiscal management. Under Cox's leadership, Charlottesville completed several large projects, including the passage of an award-winning mixed-use zoning ordinance; pedestrian-oriented development; new residential infill; mixed-income, higher-density housing; and the design of a federally funded parkway entrance into the city. As Planning Director of the City of Detroit, Cox assembled a highly talented professional and diverse team to envision and implement innovative strategies for successful urban revitalization.

Sara Daleiden is founder and director of the MKE–LAX initiative, based in Milwaukee and Los Angeles. She facilitates civic engagement through cultural exchange within developing landscapes. In Milwaukee, she engages with the Milwaukee Method of Creative Placemaking; the Beerline Trail Neighborhood Development Project; Homeworks: Bronzeville; and Designing Equity. Daleiden collaborates with the Los Angeles County Arts Commission's Civic Art as Infrastructure project, including on the documentary *Civic Art: Four Stories from South Los Angeles*. She has taught with Otis College of Art and Design's Graduate Public Practice Program.

Richard L. Hindle is an Assistant Professor of Landscape Architecture and Environmental Planning at the University of California, Berkeley. A recurring theme in Hindle's work is the tandem history and future of technology and landscape. His writing and making explore the potential of new technological narratives and material processes to reframe theory, practice, and the production of landscape. His articles have appeared in *Landscape Architecture Magazine*, UC Berkeley's *Ground Up* journal, and *Studies in the History of Gardens and Designed Landscapes*. In 2012, he received a Graham Foundation Award for the reconstruction of the "Vegetation-Bearing Architectonic Structure and Systems," and he continues to explore the technological origins of other emergent technologies. Hindle has worked as a consultant and designer, specializing in the design of advanced horticultural and building systems, from green roofs and facades to large-scale urban landscapes. He has worked with firms such as Michael Van Valkenburgh Associates, Steven Holl Architects, Rios Clementi Hale Studios, Surface Design, Shop Architects, and Atelier Jean Nouvel.

Walter Hood is the Creative Director and Founder of Hood Design Studio in Oakland, California. He is also a Professor at the University of California, Berkeley, and lectures on professional and theoretical projects nationally and internationally. Hood has been a recipient of the MacArthur Fellowship, the Gish Prize, and the 2017 Academy of Arts and Letters Architecture Award.

Hood Design Studio is a tripartite practice, working across art + fabrication, design + landscape, and research + urbanism. The resulting urban spaces and their objects act as public sculpture, creating new apertures through which to see the surrounding emergent beauty, strangeness, and idiosyncrasies. The Studio's award-winning work has been featured in publications including *Dwell*, the *Wall Street Journal*, the *New York Times*, *Fast Company*, *Architectural Digest*, *Places*, and *Landscape Architecture Magazine*.

Louise A. Mozingo is a Professor of Landscape Architecture and Environmental Planning at the University of California, Berkeley. There she is also a member of the Graduate Group in Urban Design of the College of Environmental Design and Director of the American Studies program of the College of Letters and Sciences. She was named a Richard and Rhoda Goldman Distinguished Professor of Undergraduate and Interdisciplinary Studies in 2017. A former Associate and senior landscape architect for Sasaki Associates, Professor Mozingo joined the department after a decade of professional practice. In 2009, she became the founding director of a research interdisciplinary team at the College of Environmental Design, the Center for Resource Efficient Communities (CREC), dedicated to supporting resource efficiency goals through environmental planning and urban design.

Mozingo's articles and reviews have appeared in the *New York Times, Places, Landscape Journal, Journal of the History of Gardens and Designed Landscapes, Landscape Architecture Magazine, Geographical Review,* and the *Journal of the Society of Architectural Historians.* She has contributed chapters to *Everyday America: Cultural Landscape Studies after J. B. Jackson* (2003); *Healing Natures* (2008); *Worlds Away: New Suburban Landscapes* (2008); *Creativity on the Line: Design and the Corporate World, 1950–1975* (2017); *and Infinite Suburbia* (2017). Mozingo's book *Pastoral Capitalism: A History of Suburban Corporate Landscapes* (2011) won the 2011 American Publishers Award for Professional and Scholarly Excellence (PROSE Award) in the Architecture and Urban Planning category; the 2014 Elisabeth Blair MacDougall Prize from the Society of Architectural Historians for the best book in landscape history; and an American Society of Landscape Architects Honor Award for Communications in 2014.

Mozingo has been the recipient of Harvard University's Dumbarton Oaks Fellowship for Studies in Landscape Architecture; the Council of Educators in Landscape Architecture Award of Recognition for Excellence in Teaching, Writing, and Service; and the UC Berkeley Chancellor's Award of Recognition for University and Community Partnerships. She has lectured widely.

Lewis Watts is a photographer, archivist/curator, and Professor Emeritus of Art at the University of California, Santa Cruz, where he taught for fourteen years, and, before that, at the University of California, Berkeley. His work centers around the "cultural landscape," primarily in communities occupied by people of African descent. He is the coauthor of *Harlem of the West: The San Francisco Fillmore Jazz Era*

(2006) and *New Orleans Suite: Music and Culture in Transition* (2013). His work has been exhibited at and/or is in the collections of the San Francisco Museum of Modern Art; the Cité de La Musique in Paris; the Ogden Museum of Southern Art in New Orleans; the Oakland Museum of California; the Amistad Center for Art and Culture in Hartford, Connecticut; and the Newburger Museum of Art, in Purchase, New York; among others.

CONTRIBUTORS

BIBLIOGRAPHY

Adams, Olive Arnold. "Time Bomb: Mississippi Exposed and the Full Story of Emmett Till." Mound Bayou: Mississippi Regional Council of Negro Leadership, 1956.

Agerholm, Harriet. "What Is 'Whitelash,' and Why Are Experts Saying It Led to Donald Trump's Election?" *Independent,* November 9, 2016. www.independent.co.uk/news/world /americas/us-elections/whitelash-what-is-it-white-vote-president-donald-trump-wins-us -election-2016-a7407116.html.

Anthony, Carl C. *The Earth, The City, and the Hidden Narrative of Race.* New York: New Village, 2017.

Backstreet Cultural Museum. "About Us: History." Accessed October 30, 2018. www.backstreet museum.org/about-us/4544606754.

Baker Canal Corridor Project. www.bakercanalcorridorproject.com.

Baraka, Amiri. *Blues People: Negro Music in White America.* New York: William Morrow, 1960.

Beatty, Paul. *The Sellout.* New York: Farrar, Straus and Giroux, 2015.

Berlin, Ira. *Many Thousands Gone: The First Two Centuries of Slavery in North America.* Cambridge, MA: Belknap Press of Harvard University Press, 1998.

Block, Melissa. "Here's What's Become of a Historic All-Black Town in the Mississippi Delta." NPR. March 8, 2017. www.npr.org/2017/03/08/515814287/heres-whats-become-of-a-historic -all-black-town-in-the-mississippi-delta.

Boone, Kofi. "Disembodied Voices, Embodied Places: Mobile Technology, Enabling Discourse, and Interpreting Place." *Landscape and Urban Planning* 142 (August 2015).

Branley, Edward. "NOLA History: Congo Square and the Roots of New Orleans Music." *GoNOLA.* July 2, 2012. https://gonola.com/things-to-do-in-new-orleans/arts-culture/nola -history-congo-square-and-the-roots-of-new-orleans-music.

Brinkley, Douglas. *The Deluge: Hurricane Katrina, New Orleans, and the Mississippi Gulf Coast.* New York: HarperCollins, 2006.

Brown, Leslie, and Anne Valk, "Black Durham behind the Veil: A Case Study." *OAH Magazine of History* 18, no. 2 (January 2004).

Brown, Peter. "Strike City, Mississippi." *Anarchy* 7, no. 2 (February 1967).

Butler, Octavia E. *Parable of the Sower.* New York: Seven Stories, 1993.

Catholic Online. "St. Katharine Drexel." Accessed November 30, 2018. www.catholic.org/saints /saint.php?saint_id=193.

Chafe, William Henry. *Civilities and Civil Rights: Greensboro, North Carolina, and the Black Struggle for Freedom.* Oxford: Oxford University Press, 1981.

Chernow, Ron. *Grant.* New York: Penguin, 2017.

Christiaanse, Kees. "Curating the Open City: An Interview with Kees Christiaanse." *Places,* September 2009. https://placesjournal.org/article/curating-the-open-city/.

Claiming Open Spaces. Directed and produced by Austin Allen. Columbus, OH: Urban Garden Films, 1995.

Coates, Ta-Nehisi. *Between the World and Me.* New York: Spiegel and Grau, 2015.

———. "The First White President." *Atlantic,* October 2017.

Cole, Teju. *Open City.* New York: Random House, 2011.

Commission for Racial Justice. *Toxic Wastes and Race in the United States: A National Report on the Racial and Socio-Economic Characteristics of Communities with Hazardous Waste Sites.* New York: United Church of Christ, 1987.

Craig, Eric. "New Orleans East Residents, Activists Discuss Secession from City." *New Orleans Times-Picayune,* May 10, 2017.

Cruse, Harold. *The Crisis of the Negro Intellectual.* New York: William Morrow, 1967.

The Cultural Landscape Foundation. "Middleton Place." https://tclf.org/landscapes/middleton -place#.

Dave Chappelle: "Equanimity" and "The Bird Revelation." Directed by Stan Lathan. Netflix, 2017.

David, Maria. "1974: Welcome to Uptown Charlotte's 'Great Disc.'" *Charlotte Observer,* updated August 16, 2015. www.charlotteobserver.com/news/local/article31203281.html.

Dent, Thomas. *Southern Journey: A Return to the Civil Rights Movement.* New York: William Morrow, 1997.

———. *Southern Journey: A Return to the Civil Rights Movement.* Athens: University of Georgia Press, 2001.

Destination Tips. "12 of the Worst Places to Live in the US." YouTube video, 4:09. Posted June 17, 2016. www.youtube.com/watch?v=8nGYkEBDjX8.

Deutsch, Stephanie. *You Need a Schoolhouse: Booker T. Washington, Julius Rosenwald, and the Building of Schools for the Segregated South.* Evanston, IL: Northwestern University Press, 2011.

Du Bois, W. E. B. *The Souls of Black Folks.* New York: Random House, 2003.

Ellison, Ralph. *Invisible Man.* New York: Random House, 1952.

The Equal Justice Initiative. "The National Memorial for Peace and Justice." February 28, 2018. https://eji.org/national-lynching-memorial.

Gade, Marian L., and George Strauss. "In Memoriam: Clark Kerr." University of California Academic Senate, 2003. https://senate.universityofcalifornia.edu/_files/inmemoriam/html/clarkkerr.html.

Garland, Phyl. "Atlanta: Black Mecca of the South." *Ebony,* August 1971.

Gratz, Roberta Brandes. *The Battle for Gotham: New York in the Shadow of Robert Moses and Jane Jacobs.* New York: Nation, 2010.

Green, Jared. "A New Look at the Trail Blazing David Williston." *The Dirt,* August 8, 2016. https://dirt.asla.org/2016/08/08/a-new-look-at-the-trail-blazing-david-a-williston/.

Hansberry, Lorraine. *To Be Young, Gifted and Black.* New York: Signet, 1970.

Hardy, Steve. "Engineers Hope to Open Comite River Canal in 2021: Work Isn't Just Digging a 12-Mile Ditch." *Advocate.* November 7, 2018.

Himes, Chester. *If He Hollers Let Him Go.* Cambridge, MA: Da Capo, 1945.

Hirsch, Arnold R. "'Containment' on the Home Front: Race and Federal Housing Policy from the New Deal to the Cold War." *Journal of Urban History* 26, no. 2 (January 2000).

———. "'The Last and Most Difficult Barrier': Segregation and Federal Housing Policy in the Eisenhower Administration, 1953–1960." Poverty & Race Research Action Council. 2005. www.prrac.org/pdf/hirsch.pdf.

hooks, bell. "Postmodern Blackness." *Post Modern Culture* 1, no. 1 (1990).

Horne, Frank S. "The Open City, Threshold to American Maturity." *Phylon Quarterly* 19, no. 2 (1957).

House of Dance and Feathers. Accessed October 30, 2018. http://houseofdanceandfeathers.org.

Insecure. Produced by Issa Rae. HBO series, 2016–19.

Jackson, J. B. *The Necessity for Ruins.* Amherst: University of Massachusetts, 1980.

Jacobs, Jane. *The Death and Life of Great American Cities.* New York: Random House, 1961.

Joliet Junior College. "History: First Community College." Accessed October 14, 2019. www.jjc.edu/about-jjc/history.

Joseph, May. *Nomadic Identities: The Performance of Citizenship.* Minneapolis: University of Minnesota Press, 1999.

The Julius Rosenwald Fund. *Community School Plans.* Bulletin No. 3. Nashville: Julius Rosenwald Fund, 1924.

Katt Williams: Great America. Directed by Leslie Small. Produced by Aaron Latham James, Gerald McBride, Lena Smith, and Katt Williams. Netflix, 2018.

Kerr, Clark. *The Great Transformation in Higher Education, 1960–1980.* Albany: State University of New York Press, 1991.

———. *12 Systems of Higher Education: 6 Decisive Issues.* International Council for Educational Development. New York: Interbook, 1978.

———. *The Uses of the University.* Cambridge, MA: Harvard University Press, 2001.

King, Martin Luther, Jr. "A Creative Protest." In *The Papers of Martin Luther King, Jr.,* vol. 5: *Threshold of a New Decade, January 1959–December 1960,* edited by Clayborne Carson, Tenisha Armstrong, Susan Carson, Adrienne Clay, and Kieran Taylor. Berkeley: University of California Press, 2005.

Leading on Opportunity. "Chapter 2: The Impact of Segregation." Opportunity Task Force Report. *Leading on Opportunity* (March 2017). www.leadingonopportunity.org/report /chapter-2.

Littlefield, Daniel. *Rice and Slaves: Ethnicity and the Slave Trade in Colonial South Carolina.* Chicago: University of Chicago Press, 1991.

Lopez, German. "Roy Moore: America 'Was Great at the Time When Families Were United— Even Though We Had Slavery.'" Vox, December 8, 2017. www.vox.com/policy-and-politics /2017/12/7/16748038/roy-moore-slavery-america-great.

Lowenthal, David. "Past Time, Present Place: Landscape and Memory." *Geographical Review* 65, no. 1 (January 1975). https://doi.org/10.2307/213831.

Lowery, Wesley. "Black Lives Matter: Birth of a Movement." *Guardian,* January 17, 2017. www .theguardian.com/us-news/2017/jan/17/black-lives-matter-birth-of-a-movement.

Marginson, Simon. *The Dream Is Over: The Crisis of Clark Kerr's California Idea of Higher Education.* Oakland: University of California Press, 2016.

Martin, Douglas. "A Village Dies, a Park Is Born." *New York Times,* January 31, 1997.

Martin, Justin. *Genius of Place: The Life of Frederick Law Olmsted.* Cambridge, MA: Da Capo, 2011.

McCammon, Sarah. "The Story Behind '40 Acres and a Mule.'" *Code Switch.* NPR. January 12, 2015. Audio, 3:44. www.npr.org/sections/codeswitch/2015/01/12/376781165/the-story -behind-40-acres-and-a-mule.

Mobley, Joe A. "In the Shadow of White Society: Princeville, a Black Town in North Carolina, 1865–1915." *North Carolina Historical Review* 63, no. 3 (July 1986).

Morrison, Toni. *Beloved.* New York: Random House, 1987.

Murch, Donna Jean. *Living for the City: Migration, Education, and the Rise of the Black Panther Party in Oakland, California.* Chapel Hill: University of North Carolina Press, 2010.

Naylor, Gloria. *The Women of Brewster Place.* New York: Penguin, 1983.

Newkirk, Vann R., II. "Fighting Environmental Racism in North Carolina." *New Yorker,* Jan-

uary 16, 2016. www.newyorker.com/news/news-desk/fighting-environmental-racism-in
-north-carolina.

Parry, Marc. "How Should We Memorialize Slavery?" *Chronicle of Higher Education,* August 29,
2017. www.chronicle.com/article/How-Should-We-Memorialize/241043.

Pfeiffenberger, Sylvia. "Durham's 'Black Wall Street.'" *Duke Today,* January 25, 2007. https://
today.duke.edu/2007/01/parrish.html.

Popper, Karl R. *The Open Society and Its Enemies.* London: Routledge, 1945.

Race Forward: The Center for Racial Justice Innovation. "Facing Race: 2019 Program." Accessed
October 11, 2019. https://facingrace.raceforward.org/program/full-program.

Ransom, Reverdy C. *Preface to History of A.M.E. Church.* Nashville, TN: A.M.E. Sunday School
Union, 1950.

Rosenfeld, Seth. "The Cautionary Tale of Clark Kerr." *San Francisco Chronicle,* December 4,
2003.

———. *Subversives: The FBI's War on Student Radicals, and Reagan's Rise to Power.* New York:
Picador, 2013.

Samuels, Diana. "St. George Incorporation Portrayed as 'Secession' in National Media." *New
Orleans Times-Picayune,* December 4, 2013.

Second Peace Conference at The Hague. *Signed—18 October 1907: Entry into Force—26 January
1910: Laws and Customs of War on Land, Article 25.*

Selma. Directed by Ava DuVernay. Produced by Christian Colson, Dede Gardner, Jeremy
Kleiner, and Oprah Winfrey. Los Angeles, CA, 2014.

Sennett, Richard. "The Open City." *Urban Age,* November 2006.

Sims, Alexandra. "Mannequin Challenge: Black Lives Matter Recreate Police Shootings of Unarmed Black Men." *Independent,* November 11, 2016. www.independent.co.uk/news/world
/americas/mannequin-challenge-black-lives-matter-video-police-shootings-philandro
-castile-sandra-bland-alton-a7411176.html.

Sisters of the Blessed Sacrament. "Interactive Timeline." Accessed November 30, 2018. www
.katharinedrexel.org/st-katharine-drexel-overview/interactive-timeline/.

Sobel, Mechel. *The World They Made Together: Black and White Values in Eighteenth-Century
Virginia.* Princeton, NJ: Princeton University Press, 1987.

Staples, Gracie Bonds. "Atlanta Literary Society Dedicates Toni Morrison 'Bench by the Road.'"
Atlanta Journal-Constitution, March 8, 2016. www.myajc.com/lifestyles/atlanta-literary
-society-dedicates-toni-morrison-bench-the-road/gvga31y94bqfQ6sWrOVKjM/.

Stilgoe, John R. *What Is Landscape?* Boston: MIT Press, 2015.

Strain, Christopher. "Soul City, North Carolina: Black Power, Utopia, and the African American Dream." *Journal of African American History* 89, no. 1 (Winter 2004).

The Third Man. Directed and produced by Carol Reed. Shepperton, UK, 1949.

Tuskegee Institute National Historic Site, National Park Service. "Learning from Leaders: David Williston." Last modified February 21, 2018. www.nps.gov/articles/david-williston-learning -from-leaders.htm.

United States Department of the Interior, National Park Service. "National Register of Historic Places Registration Form: Eatonville Historic District." Tallahassee, FL: Bureau of Historic Preservation, September 9, 1997. https://npgallery.nps.gov/GetAsset/e5fa60c5-551d -41d3-bbef-2a52ff3a7b0b.

———. "National Historic Landmark Nomination Form: Andrew Rankin Memorial Chapel, Frederick Douglass Memorial Hall, and Founders Library." Washington, DC: National Historic Landmarks Survey, August 2000. www.howard.edu/library/development/Historic LandmarkNom.pdf.

———. "The Rosenwald School Building Program in North Carolina, 1915–1932." In "National Register of Historic Places Multiple Places Documentation Form: Rosenwald Schools in North Carolina, 1915–1932." Raleigh, NC: Bureau of Historic Preservation, July 9, 2015.

"U.S. Decennial Census." Social Explorer. Accessed October 1, 2019. https://socialexplorer.com /explore-tables.

Van Heerden, Ivor, and Mike Bryan. *The Storm.* New York: Viking, 2006.

Vann, Andre D., and Beverly Washington Jones. *Durham's Hayti.* Charleston, SC: Arcadia, 1999.

Von Hoffman, Alexander. "Like Fleas on a Tiger? A Brief History of the Open Housing Movement." Joint Center for Housing Studies of Harvard University. August 1998. www.jchs .harvard.edu/sites/default/files/von_hoffman_w98-3.pdf.

Whitehead, Colson. *Zone One.* New York: Anchor, 2011.

Wideman, John Edgar. *Fanon.* New York: Houghton Mifflin, 2008.

———. *The Homewood Trilogy.* New York: Avon, 2008.

Wilkerson, Isabel. *The Warmth of Other Suns.* New York: Random House, 2010.

Wilkins, Craig L. *The Aesthetics of Equity: Notes on Race, Space, Architecture, and Music.* Minneapolis: University of Minnesota Press, 2005.

Wood, Peter. "'It Was the Negro That Taught Them': A New Look at African Labor in Early South Carolina." *Journal of Asian and African Studies* 9, no. 3–4.

The World, The Flesh and the Devil. Directed by Ranald MacDougall. Produced by George Englund, Sol C. Siegel, and Harry Belafonte. Los Angeles, CA, 1959.

Works Progress Administration, Project #65-32-3892.

———. "Project Proposal #1 from City of Raleigh." August 14, 1935.

INDEX

Italicized page numbers refer to illustrations. Page numbers with an "n" appended indicate a page number in notes.